HAUNTED
MANATEE
COUNTY

HAUNTED MANATEE COUNTY

LIZ REED

Published by Haunted America
A Division of The History Press
Charleston, SC
www.historypress.com

First published 2018

Manufactured in the United States

ISBN 9781467138000

Library of Congress Control Number: 2018942448

CONTENTS

ACKNOWLEDGEMENTS

The author would like to thank the following for any and all assistance. To the wonderful ladies at Bradenton Carnegie Library, thank you for all your help.

The Paranormal Society of Bradenton, Florida; it is a great team to work with.

To my brother, Robby, and sister, Janet—you kept me somewhat sane!

To Grannie Annie for her empathy and way with words.

To Ron, my husband for enjoying paranormal investigating, as much as I do. Thank you for your love and support. Love you.

To my daughter, Jamie, you went from my little redheaded tomboy to a wonderful woman. I am very proud of you. Thank you for the love and support you give me and the great job you do on our website. I couldn't do it without you. I enjoy our road trips and the investigating we do together. We need to do more road trips. I love you so much, Mum.

To Sherey Shoble, and Eileen Kuckuck for believing in me all these years. Thank you, guys! Love you both.

And finally to my son, Ricky, you moved ahead into the next life before me, which wasn't fair. But nobody ever said life was fair. I miss you with all my being and know that you are always with me. I will never forget. I can't wait to be with you again. We'll have fun haunting everyone! I love you and miss you so much, Mom.

To all my loved ones who have moved on before me: Mikey, Danny, Will, Chris, Jack, Chuck E., Mom, Dad and Lorraine. See you again. You are truly missed.

Map of Manatee County in 1856. *Library of Congress*.

INTRODUCTION

In 1856, Manatee County, Florida, covered five thousand square miles. From the Gulf of Mexico to Lake Okeechobee, it was as large as Connecticut. It was later broken up to form the surrounding counties—Sarasota, Charlotte, De Soto, Hardee, Highlands and Glade. So many of these areas, though historically a part of Manatee County, are today considered separate counties.

Explorers and early settlers found manatees (sea cows) in the local rivers, and when the state divided into counties, this area became Manatee County. The area had been inhabited by Native Americans two thousand years before explorer Hernando de Soto landed at the southern mouth of the Manatee River in the spring of 1539. As it is known, De Soto came hoping to take treasures back to Spain. On his way through Florida, he stole the Indians' food, kept some of them for slaves and killed the rest. Of the ones he enslaved, he demanded they give him directions to El Dorado, a city that he believed to be carved from and paved in gold. After several expeditions failed, he returned to Cuba.

After the end of the Second Seminole War, the area was opened for settlement in 1842 under the Armed Occupation, which allowed any head of family or single man to earn title to 126 acres of land by erecting a dwelling, cultivating five or more acres and living on the land for five years. This gave opportunity for men to settle in Florida.

Picture yourself back in the 1800s, deep in the wilderness of Florida, a place teeming with Native Americans, challenging wildlife and lots of water. That's all that is around you.

This book contains both historical legends and ghost stories, as well as stories about the investigations conducted by the Paranormal Society of Bradenton, Florida. On these investigations, we use a lot of different equipment, which will be mentioned in this book. To help you understand, here is some information on equipment we use and why. We use a DVR system to always have a camera running in the rooms so we don't miss anything. We have a full-spectrum video camera that enables you to pick up things in the spectrum of light that our eyes can't see. We have digital recorders to pick up noises and voices we may not hear or to help verify what we did here, and sometimes we use headphones to listen in real time. Several voice boxes are used, such as from a Portal, SCD-2 and Olivus. This enables a spirit to use radio frequencies to speak. A thermal camera is used to catch hot and cold spots. A cold spot will usually show up alongside a spirit presence. We use digital cameras and regular old film cameras to see if we can catch something. K2 meters and Mel meters are used to let us know if there is a change in temperature or electric field. Spirits are also able to use K2 meters to answer yes and no questions.

Manatee County Proper

Downtown Bradenton

The Money Panic of 1837 caused the loss of many plantations in the upper peninsula of Florida. In 1842, after the collapse of the Union Bank in Tallahassee, Dr. Joseph Braden and his attorney brother, Hector, came to Manatee County under the Armed Occupation Act. Passed in 1842, this act allowed settlers to claim 160 acres at a cost of $1.25 per acre to make a fresh start in Florida.

Along with the Bradens, the Gambles, the Wyatts and the Wards also came to settle this land, which would be called Bradenton. They had all served on the Tallahassee bank board and were all from Virginia. These connections may make one wonder if these families were somehow involved in that 1842 banking system collapse.

In 1843, Dr. Joseph Braden built a log cabin on Ware's Creek, five miles from the mouth of the river, on the site near the present-day Asbury Towers. For the next three years, they struggled to make their homestead succeed. This difficulty would not discourage Joseph from building a larger plantation of the kind the brothers had dreamed about. He started out growing tobacco but discovered it wasn't as profitable as sugarcane. So, he changed to sugarcane and planted it all along the Manatee River, where it met the Braden River. He found that a sandbar in the river prevented larger boats from reaching his sugar mill. Joseph then went on to build

Old Main Street in 1904. *Manatee County Library.*

a pine log pier in the deeper channels of the Manatee River, where the present-day Old Main Street is located. This pier burned to the ground in 1878, causing one man's death.

To protect his investments from Seminole attacks, he built a stockade in the late 1840s with loopholes for the riflemen. Right next door to the stockade, Joseph built a two-story building that had a trading post on the first floor and living quarters on the second floor. It was then named Fort Braden.

In 1851, Joseph built a lavish home that came to be known as Braden Castle. The castle survived Indian attacks, hurricanes and the harsh summer heat. It is reported that Chief Billy Bow Legs attacked the Castle, taking two mules and a few slaves. He returned them the following day, however, saying that he did it just because he could get away with it.

Life moved on in the new town, as both families and industries began to grow. The Watts were involved in bringing slaves from the Keys with Hector Braden to sell in the area. Around this time, slavery was supposed to have been abolished, but here in the South it still went on.

In 1857, Joseph was in such debt that he lost Fort Braden, Braden Castle and everything else he owned, including any slaves and other assets he had acquired. He left Manatee County and returned to Tallahassee. He's said to be buried in Galveston, Texas. The castle ended up burning to the ground in a horrible fire, but its ruins still mark where it stood. There is a rumor of ghostly activity on the old grounds of Braden Castle. The ruins, however, are in the middle of a mobile home park, so no one can do any investigating to see if the rumors are true. Some longtime residents of the trailer park say that at certain times of the year, they can smell the lingering aroma of burning embers.

Hector, in contrast to his brother, was a smooth-talking ladies' man who loved his smuggled Cuban rum and employed French phrases to woo women. He never married, and as far as we know, he had no children or immediate descendants.

On October 14–15, 1846, one year after Florida became a state, a hurricane came through and sucked the Manatee River so dry that deer could walk across it, just as it would many years later, in September 2017, when Irma came through. They didn't know back then that a hurricane had an eye; they thought that the calm was just a break between two storms. When Hector Braden was returning to Manatee by horseback and was caught in the storm, after the first part of the hurricane passed he decided it was safe for him to continue. But it was only the eye. As Hector crossed the riverbed, his horse got stuck in quicksand-like mud. While his mount struggled against the muck, the back end of storm tore through, bringing a torrent of water back into the river.

Legend has it that the following day, they found Hector still sitting on his horse with his eyes wide open, still holding the reins. Both horse and rider were dead. He was buried on the riverbank. A letter was sent to his family in Virginia telling them of the horrible tragedy and where Hector's body was buried, but it is unknown whether they came to claim him or move his body. Locals say that they can sometimes hear the clopping of horse hooves and believe it to be Hector riding his steed down toward the river that fateful night.

Hector is also known to hang out on a certain corner of the street in the downtown area. Of course, he's not far from libations and the bars. He loves to talk to you if you happen on by. You may feel a cold touch, get shivers on your neck or think that you hear a voice. That's Hector trying to get your attention. He is known to trick you into asking a question, but don't fall for it. If you ever find yourself standing on Hector's corner, please don't ask the question, "Would you like to have a drink?" Hector will take you up on that offer and follow you until he gets his drink. He will make always make you aware of his presence somehow to let you know that you still owe him a drink. If you find yourself in this predicament, you need to go to a local bar on Old Main Street and buy two drinks—one for you and one for Hector. Enjoy your drink, but leave Hector's alone on the bar. He's a crazy spirit that must have been a character in life.

Shoppers on Old Main. *Manatee County Library*.

The building on Hector's corner has apartments on the top floor. One of the tenants told me that Hector likes to open and close her cabinets, but if she places a shot of rum on her counter, he will stop. Hector doesn't wander too far from his favorite area unless he heads to the bars trying to collect on those drinks he's owed.

In 1870, Major Turner petitioned for the community to have its own name and post office, and eight years later, it became Braidentown. Helen Warner, acting as secretary, misspelled the name, and for twenty-seven years, it stayed as Braidentown. In 1904, the *i* ,was dropped, and it became Bradentown. In 1924, the *w* was dropped, making it Bradenton at last—finally correctly named after our founding fathers.

As of yet, I've been unable to find any pictures of Joseph and Hector, but I would love to see what they looked like.

Pier 22

Pier 22 was built in 1928, dedicated to twenty-one men who paid the ultimate price serving in World War I. Over the next fifty years, the building would be used for a variety of functions. The second floor was used for USO dances, and the first floor was used as a warehouse for freight from steamers coming up the river. At one point, it's said to been used as a triage hospital for wounded soldiers. Then a part of it became South Florida Museum's first home and the first home in Manatee County for Snooty the Manatee. He was kept right there on the river.

When the museum benefactors constructed their new building, they built an aquarium area where they could keep Snooty. Snooty could never be returned to the wild, as he had been born in captivity and his mother died, so he never learned how to survive on his own. Snooty was the oldest living manatee in captivity.

The Manatee County Chamber of Commerce also resided there for thirty-four years, along with Manatee County's first radio station, WTRL, which started broadcasting in 1946.

In 1974, the Miller family acquired the building on the pier. After two years of restoration and preserving the old building's Spanish style, it was opened as Pier 22 restaurant. The top floor is a private rental area, and it's known

Aerial view of downtown Bradenton. *Manatee County Library.*

Pier 22. *Manatee County Library.*

for the lights turning off and on at random times. The employees state that they hear music from earlier times, as well as people having conversations. The sound of dancing is heard going on all the time when the upstairs is not in use, and the clinking of glasses is often heard.

The tower of the building was used for Bradenton's first radio station, WTRL. The disc jockey who hosted the talk radio show at night told me that it was a very creepy building but not scary to him. Although he knew he was the only one there, he could hear the conversations, dancing and music all night. After a while, he became so used to it that he felt like he had company in the building. This is what is called a residual haunting, as it plays over and over again just like a recording, continuously reliving the past.

While eating in the restaurant area downstairs, people have reported having had an ice-cold feeling brush against them or someone touch or poke them. When they turn to see who it is, no one is there. This is believed to be the spirits of soldiers who didn't make it home.

South Florida Museum

When South Florida Museum moved from the pier to its current location, it had more space to display artifacts. New dioramas included such antiquities as physicians' tools and Native American artifacts. Employees have told me that they've experienced weird feelings of being watched or felt a cold burst of air brush past them. These sensations create a feeling of total discomfort around these items at times.

If you look down Old Main Street (12th Street), from 3rd Avenue, you notice a grading slope as it goes down to the river. Where the slant begins is where the first pier stood in 1878. In a horrible tragedy, it burned to the ground, killing one man. All the land that is there today was dirt fill from the local Native American burial grounds. Some of the artifacts that the museum displays today came from those burial grounds. This may explain the feelings that employees get from the relics.

Right there on the two corners where the pier started, there once stood two buildings. One was the first store, which twenty-two-year-old Robert Beall Sr. opened in 1915, a dry goods store called the Dollar Limit. His family members still own the Bealls Company and the department stores that are located all throughout the state.

There was also the Garr House, on the corner near where the Bradenton Herald Building is today; it is a parking lot now. It was the oldest wooden building in Bradenton and known to be a boardinghouse. There is a story that a woman staying at the Garr house was said to be murdered by another woman. It is said they both were women of ill repute. The spirit of the murdered woman wanders the parking lot, and she's been heard saying that she was killed over money. The crime is unsolved, so it seems the other woman was never arrested or charged with the murder and walked away free.

Snooty the Manatee, the county's beloved mascot, had a tragic accident on July 23, 2017, and passed away at the age of sixty-nine. A birthday gala had just been held in his honor. People came from all over the state and world to see this gentle creature. A trapdoor leading to the plumbing area somehow was pushed opened, leaving a dangerous opening in the bottom of the viewing tank. The smaller manatees were able to enter and exit, but Snooty, being as big as he was, could not turn himself to get back out. Manatees, like humans, need air to breathe, and Snooty was unable to surface to get air. I'm sure his spirit will be felt around there forever. We will miss this wonderful manatee that kept us smiling throughout the years and died in such a tragic way.

The Play

The Play, a local arcade and bar, was originally the Bradenton Publishing Company. Its biggest client was the *Manatee River* newspaper, which was published from this site from 1922 to 1935. When the newspaper went out of business, so did the publishing company.

The building is located on Old Main Street in downtown Bradenton. The current owner is Joey Bennett, and it is now the largest bar downtown. Before the Play moved in, the building housed several different businesses over the years. It became a cigar bar in 2007 and then the Fish, a sushi bar. When Joey Bennett purchased the property in 2016, he had the top floor gutted to make room for office space or rental apartments. Since the construction began, it has stirred up the energy lying dormant in the old building.

The second floor has a few spirits up there. One is a gentleman who died in 1915 and has been documented over a voice box saying, "He wasn't a doctor but he did illegal procedures on women." Imagine a time when frightened young women had nowhere to turn but backstreet butchers. At that time, before the courthouse was built in 1913, the top floors of the buildings on Main Street were considered "seedy" hotels. This specter has been seen walking around upstairs, watching the activities of the living. Employees get a creepy feeling, like they are being watched, when they have to go up there. Items move around on their own, and whispering is heard.

This spirit is sometimes seen looking out the windows at passersby. Other shadows have also been seen up there, and you always get a feeling of being watched from across the street. Just take a look up at the windows and you may catch a ghostly figure looking back at you.

Downstairs, there is a woman named Alexandria that sits at the fourth-to-last bar stool. At the time of our investigation there, Robert, who is the manager and one of our investigators, made her a margarita. Kenny, another investigator, went to put a piece of equipment next to the drink, and we could hear a woman's voice saying, "Don't touch" with our own ears. Needless to say, she thought that Kenny was going for her drink. Kenny wasn't allowed near that seat or drink the rest of the night, as she would get upset.

It is rumored that she was waiting for a man who never showed up, and she's said to have jumped from one of the top-floor windows of one of the buildings on Old Main Street after her gentleman never came to meet her. So, if you happen to be seated in that chair or next to it and hear a woman

The Play. *Author's collection.*

saying, "Don't touch," that will be Alexandria. If you tell Rob that you heard it, you'll get a big smile and a chuckle from him.

While working at his desk in an upstairs office near the security camera monitor, Rob has also seen a man in a white outfit come into the establishment and sit down at the bar. He has gone down to serve him at the bar but found no one there. He asked the chef who was working in the kitchen downstairs where the man went, and the chef told him that no one had come in.

During business hours, they've had a whole stack of glasses (twelve to fifteen) violently thrown off the shelf so hard that it hit the glass beer cooler on the other side of walkway behind the bar, almost six feet away. Orbs have been seen with the naked eye moving around, and at times when it's quiet, you can feel the presence of someone trying to talk to you but you can't understand what they are saying.

The spirits do not seem to bother anyone, but they do try to get your attention pretty strongly at times. They just seem to want to see what is going on. The building has gone through a lot of changes in the past few years, and they are just watching to see if they approve of the changes.

Old Bakery Building

The old "Bakery Building" is located on Old Main Street in downtown Bradenton. It was built in 1910 and housed the Bradenton Board of Trade on the second floor. Its original façade still stands today. A name for the bakery was never recorded, but locals recall stories from their grandparents. The ovens were located in a single-story attachment on the southwest corner of the parking lot. It helped to keep the interior building cooler since there was no air conditioning at the time.

I have heard stories from people who told me that their parents and grandparents were frequent customers there, and they said the bakery made the greatest orange cream puffs and the absolute best chocolate cake in Bradenton.

The top floor was the office and was relegated to the Board of Trade and bank officials. Over the years, the building went on to become the Union Bus Station in 1926 and the Yellow Cab Company, as well as several printing companies in the 1930s. The last recorded tenant was Carousel Antiques in 1977, and now it has sat vacant for many years.

Some people recall that the baker's name was Dave and that he was most known for his moist and delicious chocolate cake. One of the bank officials loved Dave's chocolate cake so much that he would send his wife down to the bakery to pick one up when he had a taste for it, which was quite often. Dave and the bank official's wife fell in love. The bank official discovered the secret tryst and allegedly had Dave killed. As Dave will tell it, verified in our EVPs (electronic voice phenomena) found on electronic recordings that are interpreted as spirit voices, "She was the love of my life." But watch it ladies: he is known to flirt with other woman still today. Dave will also tell you that "he made the best chocolate cake in Bradenton and that the recipe died with him." In multiple EVP sessions, he has only revealed one ingredient: lard. This must be what made his cake so moist.

Sometimes, when standing in the parking lot area behind the old Bakery Building on Main and Third, the scent of cinnamon or freshly baked bread will suddenly fill the air. But if you try to find the source of the delicious aroma, there's nothing there. Dave is still working.

There are a few other spirits there, like Catherine, who loves to have music played for her; ABBA is one of her favorites. We do know that she has a love for one of our old tour guides, Kyle, as he along with one of our team members discovered her; he was the first one with whom she would communicate, via a K2 meter. A spirit can illuminate the lights on

The old Bakery Building. *Author's collection*.

Orb caught at the old Bakery Building. *Author's collection*.

the device in answering yes or no questions. They could also hear her voice. Her presence is strongly felt throughout the room. She would now and then come out to the parking lot and let us know that she was upset with Kyle for not coming back to see her. There is also an eight-year-old boy, named Samuel, who likes to talk about stickball. He has been caught on a digital recorder saying his name. He loves to say he was the pitcher and made a lot of scores. When children are around, he becomes very active, trying to get their attention. We think he just wants to start up a game and play with them. From our investigations, we have learned that the spirits of his father, Alex, and mother are also present. They lived in Manatee County in 1850. Historical documents show they were one of the families who tragically drowned in the river that year. The county dredged the Manatee River in 1850 and left a lot of deep, inconspicuous areas along the coast of the river, and about one hundred people drowned that summer. Bathers would unknowingly get in these deep areas, not know how to swim well and drown.

There is also an older male inside the bakery that likes to play hide-and-seek. He goes from room to room, making you look for him. We have seen him dart around and tease us to find him.

Then there is Rose, a woman with such a tragic story. We have confirmed with Rose through multiple EVP sessions that her story is as follows. Rose and her husband had been overindulging at a local bar. They were sitting in their parked car outside at a bar on Main Street arguing. They had their nine-month-old daughter with them strapped in her carrier seat. Rose's husband told her that he was too drunk to drive them home, so Rose insisted that she was fine to drive instead. Rose got behind the wheel of the car and ended up hitting four parked cars, killing her daughter and her husband. She fell into a deep depression and later committed suicide. She remains earthbound until she lets go of her guilt for killing her family.

The Bakery Building still stands today and is currently being remodeled into a Mexican restaurant called La Mesa by Joey Bennett, who owns the Play. Even though Joey says he is not a believer, he is having us keep an eye on the activity at both the Play and La Mesa to make sure that all the spirits there remain content.

With all this remodeling going on, the spirits are becoming very active. Any drastic structural changes are known to activate or upset those that came before us. As a matter of fact, the whole downtown Main Street has become very active lately, as quite a few buildings have been seeing renovations. Stop by and have a meal with the old baker, Dave, play some music for Catherine or have a chat with Samuel about stickball and the other spirits that hang around there. They can be very talkative at times, as we have documented.

Dave likes his picture taken, so you should take a few pictures while you're there too. You may catch an orb or shadows in your picture, but you'll know Dave when you see him. He shows up as an outline of a face with a fancy handlebar mustache.

FROM AN INTERVIEW WITH KIM AND BRANDON BASSETT, PARANORMAL ENTHUSIASTS

There is a very old bakery building in downtown Bradenton with a lot of history. There seems to be several spirits that inhabit the building. Some are shy, but others seem to enjoy interacting with us. We were doing some investigations one night and trying out a new piece of equipment. It had an energy meter as well as a word bank. With a little practice, a spirit can manipulate the equipment to make one of the words appear on the screen. We had been getting some responses with the K2 meters and word dictionary, but nothing really firm. Then, all of a sudden, the words insects biting came up, and then another investigator picked up his cellphone and it was covered in ants.

Later, I was standing with one of our ghost tour operators, Kyle. To try and elicit response, I began asking silly questions. At one point, I asked, "What do you think of Kyle?" The meter immediately went to red, and "dork" appeared on the word bank! We all had a good laugh, and I hope the spirits did too.

Riverfront Theatre

In 1953, Dr. W.D. Sugg and Edward and Lillian Bishop graciously provided startup funding for the Riverfront Theatre. An undeveloped piece of land on the Manatee River was leased from the city for fifty years for one dollar per year. Construction began within weeks. The total cost of the building was $60,000. It was the first community theater in Bradenton.

It opened in December 1953, with the first performance being *I Remember Mama*. Over the next sixty years, the Manatee Players group would produce some of best live theater in Southwest Florida at the Riverfront Theatre. Hundreds of signatures from dozens of actors who had performed on the stage over the decades graced the walls backstage. Families performed together, and some couples became engaged and married on the stage.

To get to the control booth, you had to climb up a straight ladder and through a square hole. Staff jokingly called it the "birthing canal." After sixty years of performances, the theater became too small for the group to grow, and fundraising began for a new building. Some of the backstage signatures were removed and taken to the new theater, located not far away at 502 3rd Avenue West, but some were left behind. The old theatre was cramped; the roof leaked it and had mold problems. In 2016, the structure was torn down, and a hotel is currently being built where it once stood.

Staff and actors will tell you that it was undoubtedly haunted. They knew it from day one. A little girl, most likely the child of an actress, would hide in the women's dressing area, and they could hear her crying. The little girl liked to have her picture taken and showed up in photographs as a mist or fog. When the old theater was still there, you would occasionally see a little girl run by the front doors in a long white dress, her long hair flowing with a ribbon tied in it. There was also a couple in colonial clothing seen dancing on the stage with a cat.

Our paranormal group was the last to enter the building before it was torn down. You immediately got the feeling of being watched by a lot of people. If you were lucky, you might have heard a voice or two. I sat down onstage and saw next to me a pair of men's dress pants and dress shoes from the knees down. The rest of the figure was invisible to the naked eye. I was yelling at my husband, Ron, and another investigator who were watching me on a DVR system. They wouldn't answer, so I got up and saw them both staring at the monitor with their mouths open. They were able to see the complete body of the man walk across the stage and stand next to me the whole time I was sitting there. He was ready for his performance.

Upstairs we saw a cat walk past us across the room, plain as day, and then disappear when he got right in front of us. We saw it with our own eyes. We looked everywhere and never found a cat in the building. When we asked, the theater manager told us they did have a spirit of a cat that lived there. It seemed to be the theater's "house" cat, and when it passed away, its ghost stayed on.

Shaman Jeff Wheeler, from the Village of the Arts' Village Mystic store, also had an experience. Upon entering the stage area, he saw a couple dancing on the stage. He asked if he could help them but got no reply. He asked again, and the woman said, "He can see us." The man then came right up to Shaman Jeff's face and said, "I will kill you." Shaman Jeff told the man to go ahead and to jump in him—that he wouldn't like where he would take him. After he said that, both spirits disappeared.

This theater was built on the area where they used Native American burial grounds as landfill. The three spirits remain on the land, along with a few others. Since they have disturbed the land again by beginning construction of a nine-story hotel, the spiritual activity has become more frantic than ever. There are now at least eight spirits there, one being Native American. He is seen looking at you from around the corners of the structure they have built so far. The others are just wandering around the property looking for their familiar theater. They will show up as a mist or foggy-looking figure. I can't wait for the new hotel to open; I might be the first one to check in.

The Historical Courthouse

The historical courthouse was built in 1913, after the existing wood-frame courthouse built in 1859 became insufficient to meet the needs of the growing county. The old wooden court was described in the *Manatee River Journal* as an "inefficient and unsightly structure," and it was subject to frequent jailbreaks.

County commissioners felt that it was important to build a new, modern courthouse. Falls City Construction out of Kentucky won the bid at a price of $97,445.

The new courthouse would only be sufficient for the county's needs for a little more than a decade. Three additions were built over the years. Although the interior has changed over time, the exterior looks much as it did more than hundred years ago. Gracing the entrance at one time were a fountain and a pond home to several alligators. No record exists of how many unfortunate visitors were bitten. On top of the courthouse sat a green dome called "the skylight." It was removed in 1926, as it was a considered a fire hazard.

Three legal hangings took place on this property. In 1901, Edward Lamb was hanged for the murder of Dave Kennedy. Mr. Lamb went to talk to Mr. Kennedy about Kennedy's son bullying his son and demanded that the young man be punished. Kennedy said it wouldn't happen again, but the argument became very heated. Lamb pulled a knife on Kennedy. Kennedy was a bigger man than Lamb and was able to knock him to the ground and get the knife away from him. Kennedy wouldn't let Lamb up off the ground until he promised he would drop the argument. Lamb agreed, but as soon as he went home, he grabbed his shotgun and went looking for Kennedy. He found him at a sawmill near Braden River. With several men watching, he

The courthouse at night. *Author's collection.*

shot Kennedy and then walked closer and shot him again at such close range that his clothes caught fire.

Lamb was the only one who was hanged inside the courthouse building itself, the only white man to be hanged in Manatee County and the first white man to be hanged in the state of Florida. Lamb was hanged in the jail, which was on the top floor of the courthouse. The hood was placed over his head and the trapdoor opened, but things didn't go too well. The noose slipped off his neck after the initial *snap* of the rope. The fall didn't kill Lamb, and he was brought back up to the gallows unconscious and hanged again, which led to his death.

Another version to this story states that Lamb was hanged from the rafters of the skylight. The executioners had cut the rope a little too long, and when he was pushed from the rafters, he dropped straight into the kitchen, his feet landing in a pot of boiling water. It took twenty-eight minutes for them to get him down.

In 1907, Mr. Will Miles was next to meet the hangman's noose in Manatee County. Miles was caught in the act of attempted home invasion and burglary. Miles stabbed homeowner Anna Palmer thirteen times and then murdered her six-month-old daughter. Miles went on to rape and beat a thirteen-year-old girl, who later died of her injuries. His crimes were so heinous that he was held in Jacksonville until the trial for fear of retaliation. Mr. Miles was called the "Big Brute" by the *Manatee River Journal-Herald*. At his hanging, when brought out of courthouse, he was said to have started singing "Jesus Walk with me." His had been the trial of the century in this area, and everyone within five thousand square miles had traveled days to come see this hanging. Two armed guards were stationed around the courtyard. Just as Miles reached the scaffolding, it started to rain. They stopped the hanging and took Mr. Miles back into the courthouse. Miles continued his singing all the way back in to the courthouse. The crowd outside became very upset at the rain delay. Of course, this being Florida, fifteen minutes later, the rain dried up. Miles was brought back out of the courthouse still singing "Jesus Walk with Me." They placed the noose around his neck and dropped him, but his neck did not break. It took a full eighteen minutes for him to die, and he sang until the end. "Big Brute" Miles has been heard walking around the courthouse grounds still singing "Jesus Walk with Me."

According to papers from the Carnegie library in Bradenton, Manatee's last hanging took place in 1911. Mr. Stubs was hanged for robbing and killing his uncle. After 1923, the State of Florida decreed that all executions would be administered by the electric chair, which was the sole method of execution in Florida until 2000.

A Confederate memorial was originally sited on the west side of the Manatee County Courthouse, provided by the Judah P. Benjamin chapter of the United Daughters of the Confederacy. It was dedicated in 1924 to the "Memory of Our Confederate Soldiers." When it was moved during renovations, the county discovered a time capsule that had been buried with it. The capsule contained a number of Confederate items, like old newspapers and other keepsakes.

In 2017, Manatee County saw a big protest at the courthouse about whether to remove or leave the Confederate memorial. It was voted and passed to leave it where it had stood for ninety-three years; however, after being informed that the protests would continue, county officials voted to have it removed. The monument was removed (with only the county board knowing it was being done) during the dark of night but toppled over and was broken during the process. Who knows what activity has been stirred up at the courthouse since the monument was moved?

People who have reported for jury duty have relayed stories as well. In the cafeteria, they would feel an ice-cold chill surrounding them. Staff members would tell them that it is just Mr. Miles. Mr. Lamb is noticed every once in a while walking through the courthouse.

The courthouse was the first concrete building in Manatee County, and it has a basement. We wonder what went on in that basement. A local informed me that there is a tunnel that goes from the old sheriff's office to the courthouse. They would have the young men held in the cells carry milk crates from the sheriff's office, through the tunnel and across the courthouse to a waiting milk truck outside. He said that the sheriff's office was making moonshine, and the prisoners were carrying it to the milk truck under the cover of night so no one knew what illegal activity was really going on.

I'd love to see if there really is a tunnel, as well as see who or what might be in down there.

Hampton Inn

Although the project was initially conceived as a "ritzy playground for the roaring '20s," the high-roller hopes for the Manatee River Hotel (aka the Pink Palace) quickly sank into the gutter when the Great Depression hit and never recovered.

The hotel opened in 1925. It had 250 rooms, and each room was well appointed and had a Murphy bed. As stated in the *Manatee River Journal-Herald* on July 9, 1925, "Rendered in Italian Renaissance style it will be one of the most imposing structures in the entire state." The rooms rented for $2.25 per night, which would be just a little over $30.00 today. It would be nice to get a room rate like that nowadays! The Hampton Inn that currently occupies this spot has 119 rooms and runs a little higher than $225 per night.

At the time the hotel was opened, African Americans were not welcomed as customers. If they were part of a band slated to perform, African American performers had to leave the building as soon as their show was done, using the back service entrance and exit. I wonder if any spirits have returned to finally to enter the hotel without feeling unwelcome?

The top of hotel was where the action was. Dances were held up there, and of course drinks flowed freely—all with a gorgeous view of the Manatee River in the desired climate of Florida. A lot of famous people were drawn to the hotel, like Greta Garbo, Clark Gable, Babe Ruth and President Herbert Hoover. It is said that even Al Capone enjoyed visiting there. Capone was known to travel back and forth from Miami to Bradenton. At the time, we

Hampton Inn. *Author's collection.*

Manatee River Hotel, with the original staircase and the mailbox. *Author's collection.*

had natural mineral springs, known to some as the fountain of youth, and his doctor believed that it would help cure his syphilis. Unfortunately, with the progression of his disease, the springs were not the cure-all he had hoped for. He also invited his friends and cronies and would do some business around the area. In 1966, the hotel closed due to the poor economy.

From March 1966 to August 1966, the building became the River Hotel Senior Home, but after that short-lived venture, the spot remained vacant until 1993, when it reopened as the River Park Residence Hotel/Senior Vacation Center. A lot of mysterious things have been reported happening by people who either work or stayed there.

While working on the building, some laborers stayed in the building and started messing around, trying to get things to happen or would try playing jokes on others. For instance, while trying to play a trick on a coworker, one employee led him to a room. As they entered, books went flying across the room and furniture moved. Of course, the first employee was blamed for having things rigged, but he swore that he had nothing to do with it. Further investigation revealed no sign of tampering, and he was just as shaken as the other employees. He began to wonder if his pranks had upset something in the building.

Residents staying on the second floor would complain that the orchestra had played too late into the night before, as they could hear it. No orchestra had played in this building since the hotel closed in 1965. The complaints continued, and after a while, everyone just got used to it.

When management began to do work on the towers, none of the repairs seemed to take. Plaster would fall off the wall, and the flooring would buckle; workers in the process of renovating rooms would find their supplies scattered in disarray. Exhausting time and manpower, the owners finally gave up doing any work on the towers and left them abandoned.

Residents on the fourth floor claimed to see and hear children running down the hall from south to north and then disappear into the north-end suites. They were said to be a little boy dressed in an Easter church outfit and a little girl in a white dress. This was a common complaint and would continue until a staff member would come up and check to see if they saw them. No children were found, and the children were never even seen by the staff.

There was a female resident of the senior apartments who was said to be the meanest, nastiest person around. Nothing the staff did for her was good enough. She had a complaint about everything. But every day at 4:00 p.m., she would come down to the empty dining room, sit down at a table, turn her coffee cup over and have a conversation with two children. Now, no one could see the children, but she would tell the staff they were there. After her time talking to the children, she would then get up and return to her room. The staff said that after her conversation time with the children she was the happiest person in the world.

One night, a staff member staying at the center alone heard a loud sound coming from the north stairwell. He said that it sounded like someone banging on a railing with a pipe wrench. He was on the seventh floor when this happened, so he walked to the stairwell, looked down and yelled, "Stop it!" The noise stopped, but he decided to walk down the stairwell to see what had been going on anyway. When he reached the third floor, he felt the strangest sensation that he had passed someone and then felt himself being roughly shoved into the wall. The noise then started up again. What he heard was the sound of someone was running down the stairs after him. He fled down the stairs in a panic and called 911. The police came, but after a complete search of all the stairwells and building, no one was found.

After the Senior Vacation Center had been opened for a while, a depressed gentleman resident managed to get up to the rooftop and jumped. The building was sold, and the new management company came in and ordered all 105 senior residents to relocate immediately. It planned on making forty upscale condo units with the building once the seniors had left the property. With the housing market crash and economic failure of 2008, the project never materialized, and the property was foreclosed on. Since the city had an unpaid lien on the property, it came in, secured the building and put a chain link fence around it. The Pink Palace was now just a run-down landmark of times gone by, sitting dilapidated and empty for years.

In 2013, the Hampton Inn came in and saved the building, restoring it to what it is today. It kept the original staircase going from the first to the second floor, renovated the old restaurant area into the meeting room and kept some of the old fixtures in the décor. It even kept the old mailbox slot and is still using it today. The only difference on the outside is that the building is no longer flamingo pink.

These days, a woman in white has been spotted haunting the fourth and seventh floors. She's been known to move workers' equipment and even heavy boxes of tile. When the contractors were working on the Hampton Inn and would come to work in the morning, they would find equipment moved to different places or even different floors. We wonder if she didn't like the noise; perhaps she was a lady who partied on the top floor and had a hangover.

During the time it was closed, the police would get regular calls that lights were on in the building when there was no electricity even connected to the site. They had to do sweeps of the building. No officer would tell me the cause. They would say that "they didn't care for that building" or, "You don't want to know." A watchman is heard jingling keys and whistling in the main lobby during the night, and Al Capone has been seen riding in the elevator since the Hampton Inn has opened. It is rumored that a gun etched with the initials "A.C." was found along with an old ledger book from the hotel. Supposedly, there is a signature of Al Capone's signed in as a guest, but no one has brought it forth to authenticate. I have doubts on the gun belonging to Capone, as I don't think a gangster would put his initials on a gun.

Employees have recently told me that the sixth floor has become very active. The elevator doors will almost close and then reopen, like the safety is tripped and no one is there. This happens several times until the employee says, "Stop it, I have work to do!" Then the elevator will then go back to its normal operation.

Hampton Inn elevators, where Al Capone was said to have been seen. *Author's collection.*

There is also a spirit in the kitchen area that they have fondly named Annabelle. She's known to move things around and hide things from employees until the item suddenly reappears. When you are alone in the kitchen, she loves to push the button on the automatic paper towel machine until it all rolls out. Employees usually shout out, "That's enough, Annabelle," but she will continue until the roll is completely empty.

People staying there are starting to report that they feel like they are being watched while in their beds at night. Some have said they will wake up having the feeling that someone is sitting on the bed. It's also been reported that when the building was closed, the fire department used the building for training exercises. While in the left stairwell, firemen would step up to the fifth step and feel like they hit a brick wall. The hose became extremely heavy, and firemen reported that it felt like it took forever to get to the seventh floor. On the way back down, the sensation stopped as soon as they stepped on the fourth step.

I had never heard this story until a week after staying there, so when it happened to me and another investigator, we knew it was something to look into. When we got to the fifth step, our meters started going crazy; it made us wonder what it was all about. Then, the following week, I interviewed a fireman who also experienced it. He said they used the stairways for training, running the hoses up and down the stairwells, and the same thing happened to his crew that had happened to us twenty years later. We were blown away.

While it was a senior apartment building, the nurses on duty would stay in small apartments on the top floor. One nurse is said to have gone crazy, and she lived above the north end on the top floor above the active stairwell. It seems that when it was a senior apartment building, a woman was renting room 327. She was known to wear a strong perfume. When she passed away, they had to bleach and strip everything down in her room and then repaint everything. They redid the wooden floors. The same perfume smell came right back after they finished. Strangely, if it was a full moon, the smell got stronger. They could not rent this room out, so they ended up using it for storage. Sometimes you get a scent of strong perfume while walking on the fourth floor.

I did some research and was able to find out that some of the wood used in the inner structure of the building is from an old shipwreck from off the coast of Africa. Even though the seventh floor wasn't ready to be used, it still had to be monitored by the staff, and they would get an eerie feeling walking around on that floor.

Elevator companies would come out to do repairs, go upstairs, come down quickly and quit after going up to the elevator mechanics room. They would refuse to return to the building with no explanation. The employed maintenance people then had to take over to keep things going. When they would go up to the center tower of the building, the old hanging utility light installed there was known to start swinging on its own. Maintenance workers reported an overall creepy feeling. They refused to go up there by themselves, using the excuse that it is a high-voltage area and they needed someone there just in case something happened.

In the pipe casing in the walls of the building were found old baseball cleats, pocket watches and wallets, as though someone just dumped them in the walls to hide them and then sealed it off.

One electrician ventured to the mechanics room to go do his repair work, came back down after a short time and complained that someone was turning his lights over. He walked off the job, leaving all his tools and lights behind, never to return to the building.

Staff hated to use the north stairwell, as they would get a cold feeling in between the fifth and sixth floors. Now, this cold feeling wasn't like a blast of cold air hitting them. They felt chilled from inside out, down to the bone. They would refuse to use the north stairwell and go down a different way. Everyone got such a creepy feeling in that stairwell that it became quickly known to the staff not to use it. If they did have to use that stairwell, they would run down it as fast as they could or have someone else with them.

In the laundry room, the staff would neatly fold the sheets and pillowcases, preparing them for the housekeeping carts, only to come back and find them all over the floor and turned inside out. Every few months or so, they would also hear a loud crash coming from the kitchen. Upon investigating, they would see all the sheet trays randomly strewn about all over the kitchen. Now, these trays were stacked about four feet high and weighed a few hundred pounds, so moving the sheet trays like this would have required some serious effort. They did not just fall over.

The dishwasher was always getting in trouble for putting the dishes in upside down, as they wouldn't get properly cleaned. He would swear that he put them in correctly and would tell the manager that Casper the ghost was doing it. Little did he know!

One staff member who lived there reported that one night he was awoken, to see a black shadow in his room. It then creeped up on him and sat on his chest, and he couldn't breathe until this black shadow released the pressure and removed itself from his chest.

Management totally ignored the complaints of the staff. It blew off most of these things as unreal or blamed the staff for playing pranks on one another. In the present, pictures taken of the hotel seem to catch orb activity inside and around the outside of building. Some have caught shadows of people peering out from the windows of unused rooms. At times, photos have revealed an orb streaming down the front of the building where the gentleman jumped to his death. Whether the Hampton Inn corporate management likes it or not, it will always be known as a haunted hotel. This building is full of energy, and the activity will continue for years to come. The spirits there want to make sure that you know who was there first.

Central Records Building

The Central Records Building housed the town's first telephone company, Peninsula Telephone Company. Built in 1925, the structure later became General Telephone and Electronics Corporation. Then it became Manatee County Central Records. It's now been closed for the past fifteen years due to black mold. It is condemned—not for lease or for sale.

Local legend has it that the Central Records Building staff reported to their boss that they were seeing shadow people walking around. Personal items and other things were being moved around, and they often heard strange noises. Evidence for trials would go missing, so the occasional criminal would walk free from his crime, which didn't make the county government look good. When the activity got to be too much, the staff would call a superior, and he

Central Records Building. *Author's collection.*

would let them close early and go home for the day. They had a feeling that something was always around, watching them, and disconcerting whispering voices could be heard.

If you take pictures of the two windows that are above where it looks like a garage door would have been on the east side by the parking lot, you may catch a face in the window, staring back at you. Shadows are also often seen walking back and forth between those two windows.

The front of the building had two exterior doors, on the second and third floors, but there is no staircase or balcony off these doors. Quite recently, the county painted all the windows black on the front so you can't see inside. It really makes you wonder what truly is going on in the building and why they feel the need to hide it.

Historical Village

Manatee Historical Village is located at 1404 Manatee Avenue, about one mile east of downtown Bradenton. The village is an open-air museum and includes the 1903 Wiggins store, a boat works building, a 1912 pioneer farmhouse, a smokehouse, a sugarcane mill, a barn, a church, a schoolhouse, cow hunters bunkhouse, a steam engine and our first courthouse. Each structure has been painstakingly restored to its original appearance and function.

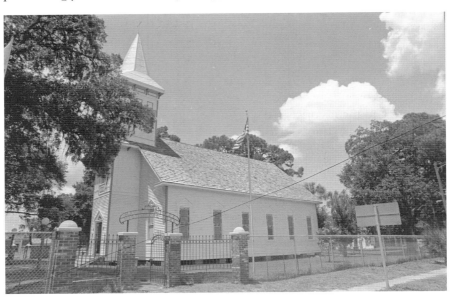

Above: Manatee County's first courthouse in the Manatee Historical Village. *Manatee County Library*.

Opposite: Old church in the Manatee Historical Village. *Manatee County Library*.

The Bunker Hill schoolhouse served the area from 1908 to 1929. It was then purchased by B.D. Galle in 1929. It served as a home for him and his daughter for sixty years. In 1989, it was moved to the historical village and restored to a one-room school. There are two doors on the old schoolhouse because boys and girls were segregated at the time and sat on different sides of the room.

Manatee County's first courthouse is also there. Built in 1859, it is the oldest surviving one-room courthouse in the state. After its function as a courthouse came to an end, it became Manatee Methodist Church and then was moved to the historical village.

Employees and visitors alike have seen apparitions in the Stephens House, the Cracker-style home that's up on short stilts. The clock has come flying off the wall in the gift shop, and guests upstairs have heard the heavy footsteps of a man. Employees have reported that it seems to happen often, and when it does, it can go on for a long time.

In the church, movements are seen up by the altar area. The cross has been turned askew, and visitors report a feeling of being watched all the time. Meanwhile, the spirits continue with their daily routines, letting guests know that they are still around.

1850 Manatee Burying Grounds

Across the street from the historical village lies the Manatee Burying Grounds.

Opened in 1850, it is the oldest cemetery in Manatee County and one of the oldest on the Gulf Coast. The land was deeded by Josiah Gates and his wife, Mary. It was closed in 1892 to all but immediate family. The last to be laid to rest there was Eva May Gates, in 1963, the granddaughter of Josiah and Mary.

There are fifteen veterans buried in that tiny cemetery—eleven Confederate soldiers and four Union army veterans—and of the Union soldiers buried there, one is Brigadier General John Riggin. He served as a colonel and aide-de-camp to Union general Ulysses S. Grant. Riggin was responsible for communicating vital information to high-ranking officers, such as General Sherman and President Lincoln's secretary of war. He was given the promotion to brevet brigadier general after the war.

In poor health from a lung injury, Riggin was advised to move to Florida. In 1886, at the age of fifty-one, he was laid to rest in the old Manatee Burying Grounds. In 1930, his wife, Fanny, was laid to rest next to him. Ironically, they are both buried by the graves of Confederate soldiers.

The 1850 Manatee Burying Grounds. *Manatee County Library.*

There are ninety-four graves that can be distinguished. Although time and weather have rendered the markers and inscriptions unreadable, their memory lives on. Many suffered through wars, hurricanes, Native American attacks and yellow fever to secure a life for their families and future generations to come.

You may feel a cold breeze or touch when you walk around this quiet resting place, and you may get the feeling you are not alone. You may feel like someone is walking along with you and hear the crunching of leaves nearby. Sometimes you will hear voices but won't be able to make out what they are saying.

Whether you take pictures during the daytime or nighttime, white streaks are known to show up, letting us know that they are still here.

FOGARTYVILLE

In 1856, after the Civil War had ended, a Gulf storm led Captain Bartholomew Fogarty and his brother John to seek protection in the Manatee River. They sailed up to a village called Manatee. They were so impressed with the area that they traveled back to Key West, collected their belongings and returned with brother William and their families.

The Fogartys established a home and boat works company under the Homestead Act of 1842. This area of Bradenton along the river became known as Fogartyville. The brothers built cypress ships that were able to withstand the turbulence of the high seas. Their business flourished in the construction of a variety of fishing and transportation vessels. After the Civil War, there was a shortage of ships, but this industrious and successful family contributed greatly to the economic restoration of South Florida.

In 1886, William and his wife donated four acres of land to be used as a burial ground. Lot prices ranged from $10 to $25 for each. The sizes of the lots varied from six spaces to twelve spaces. By 1922, the lots had all been sold. The trustees were inclined to purchase four and half more acres for $950. This was considered the Adams section.

These trustees provided an area to be set aside for those unable to purchase a burial plot. It was renamed Roger's Adam's Cemetery, after Major Allen Joseph Adam, who is buried there. In 1892, in a generous act, Garfield and Minnie Rogers donated a plot of land to the Village of Manatee. Garfield

The Fogarty family mausoleum. *Manatee County Library.*

ran the civil rights movement here in Manatee County and helped establish the first school in Manatee County for African Americans.

In 1988, both cemeteries came under the care of the County of Manatee. Between the two, there are 465 veterans buried there dating back to the Civil War.

Fogarty Cemetery

Fogarty Cemetery is known to sometimes have a mist or fog that appears in it even on the clearest of days. Pedestrians report a feeling of always being followed. While standing at the grave of a Civil War veteran and asking questions, visitors have heard a voice saying, "Back off," and people have reported being poked or touched or feeling a very cold chill go through them even on the hottest days of summer. Sometimes you may even hear the spirits having conversations.

The cemetery and the spirits are all that is left of the original family dwellings and businesses of Fogartyville. The town disappeared as bigger and better homes were built elsewhere.

Fogarty Cemetery. *Manatee County Library*.

PALMA SOLA CEMETERY

This small cemetery, located off 75th Street in Bradenton, is all that's left of the town of Palma Sola. Founded in 1886, it was for a time the largest city in Manatee County. Legend has it that a solitary palm tree at the edge of the Manatee River guided sailors to safe harbor, drawing seamen to settle in the area.

Asa Pillsbury built the church there, and in the 1800s, the Palma Sola Hotel was also constructed. Regularly filled to capacity, the hotel was the pride of a town known as a travel vacation spot.

In the 1920s land boom, big stately mansions began to be built around the area. The little quiet vacation spot disappeared, and what is left is the cemetery and church. This old cemetery holds the remains of a lot of local Cortez founding fathers, fishermen and soldiers. It's a split cemetery, and the church sits in the middle. The older part is on the left, with newer graves on the right. The gravestones come right up to the street. Many people get a spooky feeling walking through this cemetery even during the day.

You will see shadows moving around, and the smell of perfume will sometimes be noticed. It seems that the older side has a lot of restless spirits.

Palma Sola Cemetery. *Author's collection.*

You may see shadows walking alongside the church building. They will touch you somehow, and you may hear voices.

The right side has its own activity. People also hear voices, something cold may touch people around their ankles and cold chills will go through their bodies—a strange sensation in the heat of a Florida summer. A group of paranormal investigators caught three words on its voice box: "Run, hide, demon." They left right away.

To this day, some people say the atmosphere is so thick and heavy that it feels like they are hitting a strong force while searching through the cemetery and don't want to return.

CORTEZ FISHING VILLAGE

One of Florida's secrets is found one hour south of Tampa Bay: the Cortez Fishing Village. The village offers genuine historical charm as one of Florida's last operating fishing villages.

It is a small and timeless community that truly embraces its maritime heritage. No high-rises, fast-food restaurants or chain stores can be seen in this little village. It's just cottages, homes and family-owned businesses on narrow streets. Locals are proud to build or repair boats in their front yards, and crab traps are lined up ready for the next season to start. Little has changed in the last one hundred years.

The area was first settled in the 1890s, and still standing today are some of the original fishing houses that belonged to the founding families: the Bells, Taylors, Guthries, Fulfords, Greens and Moras. Selling fresh fish daily to locals, tourists and the nearby restaurants, local fishermen are sticking with a motto: "Catch to Kitchen" freshness. N.E. Taylor Boat Works is a working boat yard dating back to 1928.

The founding families originally came from North Carolina to escape the Atlantic hurricanes around 1885. They all have family still living in Cortez to this day who still continue to successfully run the family companies. Early fishermen used Skip Jackson or shallow-draft sailboats to bring in their catch. Their nets were made of natural fibers that were very heavy when wet and had to dry out between each use. Their work was demanding and dangerous. What many may not know is that some of these hardworking fishermen were women—Mada Culbreath, Mildred Moran and Rita Warden are just few. Women were not allowed on a fishing boat,

Cortez Fishing Village. *Manatee County Library.*

The Cortez schoolhouse. *Manatee County Library.*

as they were considered bad luck. These women did things on their own from the late 1920s into the 1980s.

The Cortez schoolhouse built back in 1912 is now the Maritime Museum. You will learn about the fishing community and may catch the laughter of the little kids who used to attend the old school while walking around the museum. During an investigation at the schoolhouse, we had a box that, if touched, would make a dinging noise. The spirits of the children must have loved it, as we heard that dinging all night long.

Most people don't know that the movie *The Perfect Storm* was based on the story of three fishermen from Cortez, the captain and two crewmembers. One of their widows still lives in the village.

Walking the streets of Cortez at night, you may see the shades of some of the fishermen who have lost their lives out at sea. It is a dangerous job. You might also hear the long-lost sounds of the children by the school outside playing at recess.

MANASOTA CEMETERY

In 1925, Harry Kellie and George Thacker purchased twenty-seven acres of land for use as a burial ground. A crematory was added in 1945. After Mr. Kellie's death in 1949, his widow bought out Mr. Thacker's interest. She set out to expand it and purchased sixteen more acres across the street; the funeral home and some cemetery gardens are there.

In 1958, construction on the first mausoleum got underway. Mrs. Kelley traveled throughout Portugal, Spain and Italy to find the finest natural stones, granite, marble, statues, fountains and a fancy crystal chandelier for her new mausoleums.

There are two things you will notice right away about this cemetery: the old gates as you enter and the huge pink mausoleum. The latter is the final resting place of Charles Ringling, of Ringling Brothers, and his wife and daughter, Edith and Hester. You can look through the glass door and see their tombs.

This cemetery holds the remains of a lot of famous people. Six Hall of Fame baseball players are interred at Manasota: Paul Waner, Bill McKechnie,

Manasota Cemetery *Author's collection.*

Jimmie Wilson, Johnny Cooney, Johnny Moore and Butch Henline. The "Flying Wallendas" are also buried here. The Wallendas were a circus family known for performing daring stunts on the high wire, including the infamous seven-person chair pyramid, without using a safety net. Several members of the group were killed in the tragic accident of 1962 when the pyramid collapsed during a Detroit performance. Several branches of the Wallenda family still perform to this day, including Nik Wallenda, who became the first person to cross Niagara Falls on a high wire in 2012. Members of another famous circus family, the Zacchinis, known as the "Human Cannonballs," are also laid to rest here.

This cemetery is known for sightings of shadows walking around, lots of orb activity and mysterious voices. A woman wanders around looking for "Walter," and sometimes you will hear a voice saying, "Hey you, come here." Does the spirit see you? Is it asking you to come to him, or is he calling to another spirit? Spirits have been caught on camera walking around the cemetery and peeking out from behind trees and tombstones.

The cemetery contains a Freemasonry memorial that has three chairs around it. The middle chair is always the most active. While sitting there, you will get the feeling that someone is standing behind you, and you may be touched and may hear whispering in your ear. Pictures taken have shown a bolt of light visible right next to whoever is sitting in the chair.

Two young women were sitting in these chairs eating lunch one day when they began to hear footsteps and a clanging noise. They followed the noise to the mausoleum with an irongate door. As they approached, the footsteps and clanging got louder, sounding as though someone were running a tin cup across the iron bars. Frightened, the women took off running, and their lunch went flying.

Sometimes while driving through, cars have suddenly stopped running and only restarted after a while.

FROM AN INTERVIEW WITH KIM AND BRANDON BASSETT, PARANORMAL ENTHUSIASTS

One night, I, my husband and another investigator decided to go to Manasota Cemetery to conduct some investigations. We took a couple of K2 meters and digital recorders. After about forty-five minutes, without any responses, we decided to move to a set of monuments within the cemetery. It consisted of three concrete chairs surrounding a center, rectangular structure. We each sat in a chair and began asking questions. We did not get much response at first, but then my K2 meter started lighting up. We were asking yes or no questions and seemed to be getting good responses with the meter, but no voice recordings. The readings became strong at my chair, so I stood up in case the spirit wanted my chair. My husband and the other investigator came over, and we continued asking questions. Then, I started to feel a presence behind me from behind. At first, it was just a heavy, oppressive feeling, but it got steadily stronger. It felt like an angry, threatening man was standing right at my shoulder. It was so bad that I had to quickly walk away. Neither the other investigator nor my husband felt the presence, but it was so bad that I vowed to never go back. The structures appeared to have various stone Mason symbols, similar to the Secret Societies of Masons. The Masons were strictly a male society, and we wondered if one of their spirits was angry that a woman was sitting in one of their chairs.

ANNA MARIA ISLAND

Anna Maria Island is a lovely barrier island just off the coast of Manatee County. Artifacts found on the island prove that the local Tocobaga and Caloosan tribes settled there two thousand years before the Spanish arrived in 1530.

On March 27, 1513, Easter Sunday, Ponce de León discovered land and christened it "Florida." According to legend, he visited Anna Maria Island and Longboat Key, which at the time was one long island, and gave it the name of Spain's queen. He was on a quest to find the fountain of youth. This spring was said to have the powers to give eternal youth and heal the sick, in addition to being surrounded by gold and silver. Anna Maria was named and charted long before Florida became a state in 1845.

There are three cities on the small four-mile island—Anna Maria City, Holmes Beach and Bradenton Beach—and three mayors. The first permanent resident was George Bean Sr. in 1892. He settled on the northern tip of the island, which is now called Bean Point. After George Sr.'s death in 1898, his son, George Jr., took over landownership.

Charles Roser, who invented the Fig Newton in 1891, also settled on the northern tip. George Bean Jr. and Roser partnered to form the Anna Maria Beach Company to develop the area. The company built a 678-foot pier at the end of Pine Avenue in 1911, which still stands today. They built sidewalks, laid out the streets, installed water system, built homes and also ran an icehouse. Charles's father, John, always dreamed of building a

Aerial of Anna Maria Island. *Manatee County Library.*

church in loving memory of his late wife, Caroline. He wanted to ensure that everyone could attend the church no matter what religion. In 1913, Charles built the first church and donated it to Anna Maria Island as long as it would always be a community church and not defined by any particular religion. The John and Caroline Roser Memorial Chapel is thriving and still in use today. Charles died in 1937 in St. Petersburg, Florida.

Two movies were filmed on this island: in 1948, *On an Island with You*, starring Peter Lawford and Ester Williams, and in 1998, the movie *Palmetto*, starring Woody Harrelson and Elizabeth Shue.

There used to be a small airport in Holmes Beach, from 1948 to 1973. After an accident, it was closed for fear of more.

George Bean Sr. is known to walk Bridge Street, checking out what is happening to his island. He follows you only so far and then stops and waits for you to return and rejoins you. Watch out, ladies: he likes to flirt. During a ghost walk we conducted in January 2018, George seemed to fancy one older woman on the walk in particular, even following her to the beach. We

48

all saw her standing beside us holding two gloves in her hand. We turned our head to look a different way, and the next thing we knew she was asking where one of her gloves had gone to. It was not to be found anywhere. When asked, George confessed that he took it.

The Sign of the Mermaid Restaurant

Built in 1913 on the more northern end of Anna Maria Island, the Sign of the Mermaid is a small beach cottage that's been renovated into a restaurant. In 1922, the Mermaid opened and soon became the best-known secret on the island. The Mermaid was owned by Ed Spring and his two daughters, Kelie and Serena, longtime residents of the island.

It is currently owned by Deon and Dee Mattheusis. The restaurant is known to have great food and spirit activity to match. It is famous for its award-winning key lime pie. Staff and guests have occasionally reported seeing the ghosts of a woman and young girl. They are said to play "hostess"

Sign of the Mermaid. *Author's collection.*

and wander throughout the restaurant, checking on customers and making sure they are happy. A spirit of cat is also known to be there. The owner Deon says he sees the cat curled up by the fireplace, and a lot of patrons who sit in that area say they can feel a cat rub up against them.

We were lucky enough to catch the spirit of the cat during an investigation on a thermal camera. While one of our investigators was lying down on the floor by the fireplace making a petting motion, the cat appeared on our thermal camera.

The restaurant is full of other activity. You may feel like you are being watched, see a shadow walk past out of the corner of your eye or even catch an orb in a picture.

Stop by for some of that famous key lime pie and see if the cat brushes against your legs while sitting by the fireplace. It's a cozy place for all visitors. Since Hurricane Irma came through, both piers on the north end of the island were severely damaged and are closed for repairs. They are hoping to have them repaired and reopened to the public sometime in 2018.

Holmes Beach

Holmes Beach is one of the three incorporated cities on Anna Maria Island, well known for its soft sandy beaches and glorious sunsets. The sunny shores of Holmes Beach have seen more than their share of tragedy and are home to a number of ghostly residents. Local legend has it that a female spirit roams the beach by the Bali Vista motel area during the month of August. Hotel manifests show that a couple spent their honeymoon on the island. While on their vacation, the husband went on a fishing trip and never returned. Every August, her spirit returns to look for him. A young boy who died in a house on the beach can still be heard playing in his old room, and the current owners often see him out on the beach with his dog.

Manatee Causeway

Violent crimes have made their mark on Holmes Beach as well. In 1980 Dr. Juan Dumois along with his wife, brother-in-law, two sons and daughter came to Anna Maria Island from Tampa for a two-week vacation. On August 1, Dr. Dumois and his brother-in-law, Raymond Barrows, set off for a fishing trip. The group loaded their boat and headed out to Kingfish boat ramp with Dr. Dumois's sons—Eric, thirteen, and Mark, nine—in tow.

On their return, while loading the boat onto their trailer, they saw a man with a hurt ankle pushing a bike. They stopped the truck and offered him a ride. Being the doctor that he was, Dr. Dumois told the man that they would take him to get help. He took the man's bike to load it into the back of truck and told the man to get into the back seat of the truck.

After Dr. Dumois finished loading the bike, he had just settled into the driver's seat when he heard a *pop*. He turned to see his brother-in-law slumped against the passenger window, bleeding from a gunshot wound. Just as this horrific sight registered in his mind, he turned his head to see the man shoot both his sons. The man then aimed the gun at Dr. Dumois and fired twice, killing him.

The man then got on his bike and rode down to the island. A retired police officer, Colonel Robert Matzke, heard the gunshots and went running after the man, but unfortunately, he was killed too. Only Dr. Dumois's brother-in-law survived. Someone in the area had taken pictures of the murder, but it was a new camera, and none of the pictures turned out. The killer was never found. If you are in that area on the causeway on quiet nights, you can still hear the gunshots and screams of the victims.

Hailey's Motel

On Election Night November 4, 2008, Sabine Musil-Buehler, the owner of Hailey's Motel, disappeared. For years, the police searched for her, fearing the worst. They always had their eye on her estranged boyfriend, William Cumber. Cumber had been hired to work at the motel, and the day he and Sabine met, he was arrested for arson. They became pen pals while he was imprisoned, as Sabine always believed that a person could change. In October 2008, he was released from prison and moved into her apartment, where they lived as a couple. Their relationship was quite tumultuous, but Sabine always believed in seeing the good in a person. Four years later in October 2012, he was charged with her murder.

After working out a plea agreement in 2015, he told police that the couple had had their final fight and she wanted him to leave. Cumber then admitted he choked Sabine to death and buried her under a hut on the beach. Her body was finally found and put to rest. According to local legend, she can still be seen walking the beach by the hut and Hailey's Motel.

Coquina Beach

At one time, Coquina Beach had a hotel that burned to the ground. No one was hurt in the fire, but visitors of the hotel return to wander the beach at night. This beach is known to have so much activity that you can take pictures anywhere and catch orbs.

A man dressed all in black and wearing a black hat whom they call the "Black Phantom" is seen at various times even during the day, walking from the picnic area through the trees to the beach and disappearing at the water's edge. People believe that he was one of the hotel guests.

A woman was shot in the middle of Gulf of Mexico Drive. Her boyfriend was holding her at gunpoint during the seasonal rush hour in the morning. As you get close to Longboat Key Bridge, you will see the cross on the side of the road. She is known to wander the area but will leave if a man comes up to her.

Due to the fast-moving water on the end of island and under the bridge, a lot of people have drowned, including children. Shadow people are seen

Coquina Beach at night. *Author's collection.*

walking the area at night, and voices are heard. Occasionally, you can hear a cry for help.

It's said that there are a lot of Native American burial grounds that were flattened and spread over Anna Maria and Longboat Key when they started building the vacation homes and condos. Anywhere you go on both islands, you may be walking on Native American burial grounds.

From an Interview with Kim and Brandon Bassett, Paranormal Enthusiasts

There are a number of spirits that inhabit the barrier island beaches of Manatee County, including some related to previous pirate activity. One evening, four of us went to the beach to play around with the K2 meters, voice recorder and a new app on our smartphone. The app allows spirits to pull specific words from a word bank of several thousand to show up on the screen. We had been getting some hits on the K2 meter, but nothing too consistent. Nothing conclusive had been picked up off the voice recorder either. We were trying to contact a young girl, who is believed to have been captured by the famous pirate Miguel.

When asking about how she was captured, if she escaped, what happened to the crew, etc., the word life showed up on the word bank. Four seconds later, the voice recorder captures a clear female voice say, "life." We did not capture any other voices that night until near the end of the EVP session, when a male voice was captured saying, "Go away."

Bradenton Beach/Historical Bridge Street

Historical Bridge Street was the first road to connect the mainland to the island of Bradenton Beach. It was originally called Cortez Beach, but in the late 1920s, it was changed, as the editor of the *Bradenton Herald* kept calling it Bradenton Beach. In 1952, Bradenton Beach became a city.

Construction on the bridge initially began in 1921, but due to a storm, it had to be rebuilt in 1922. The Model Ts, horses and buggies and people walking could now come out to the island without having to come by boat. The noise the vehicles made crossing the bridge was said to have sounded like gunshots.

When the road opened, Bradenton Beach was home to a post office, bait and tackle shop and the Bayside Inn. The Bayside Inn, which is now the

Bridge Tender restaurant, was built in 1917, and the bridge ended right by the front doors. This is also a spot where Al Capone was known to come to the island and frequent. There was a dance hall bar next to the Bayside Inn where Capone was also known to go to.

I was told a story about the owners finding an old chest in the upstairs part of the Bridge Tender that was said to have bones in it (believed to be human). Nothing else is known about these bones. The building is said by staff members to be very active. Things move, voices are heard and shadows are seen. The building that was the dance hall is gone, but I was told that it was used as apartments at one time and was a very active place to live in.

The building is still standing today and is now the Bridge Tender restaurant. Make sure you cross the street and take pictures of the upper level and above the roof. Shadows are seen, and orbs are caught in pictures. If only this building could talk—or maybe it can.

Across the street is the Drift Inn, which is said to have once been owned by Babe Ruth. Where the post office employee parking lot is today stood three cottages, and Ruth was known to stay there while he was in town.

Historical Bridge Street. *Author's collection.*

This page: Cortez Bridge. *Manatee County Library.*

Oar House. *From the* Bradenton Herald.

The Bistros Restaurant that stands on the corner of Gulf of Mexico Drive and Bridge Street was built in 2008. Back in the 1940s, it was first the Oar House, a pretty rough little bar that ended up burning to the ground. It then became Key West Willie's—all-you-can-eat grouper fingers! Yum. It was then torn down and rebuilt as the Sun House.

The Sun House was known to have some activity. Employees were hearing a couple fighting all the time, but no one was there. Shadows have been seen walking around, even showing up on the security system, and the alarm system was being set off for no reason. They did have paranormal group come in and do an investigation, and the site was proven to be active. The Sun House was closed, and it is now the Bistros on top and the Island Times Restaurant on bottom.

Recently, while on a ghost tour there, our equipment began to alert us to activity. We were using a voice box, and a voice was telling us to "look up" and "above." K2 meters were going off at the same time. It seems that the activity continues upstairs.

Bridge Street Condominiums was built in 2008. On January 1, 2009, Sheena Morris and her boyfriend came from Tampa to spend the holiday weekend. While they were staying in what is rumored to be room 8, the neighbors started hearing fighting going between a man and a woman. It got so bad that the neighbors called the police. When the police arrived, they

Oar House after the fire. *From the* Bradenton Herald.

found Sheena in the bathtub dead, naked, with a rope around her neck. She was in a seated position, but her rear wasn't touching the bottom of tub. The Bradenton Beach Police Department ruled it a suicide.

Her mother hired a private investigator, as she didn't believe the police, and he ruled it to be a staged suicide. They felt that it was murder. It seems that her boyfriend escaped, walking right past the police as they were arriving to the scene, and no one knew. The police did question him intensely. Because they only had circumstantial evidence, they believed he had nothing to do with her death and still concluded that it was a suicide.

I've been told by locals that people staying there will leave in the middle of the night after hearing a woman screaming, scratching on the walls and banging on the doors. Maybe Sheena just wants the truth to come out, and then she can finally find some peace.

Cortez Bridge

Cortez Bridge was built in 1967 to replace the old wooden one and put in a drawbridge for boat traffic. There had been a lot of accidents over the years and people have died, but two stories stand out.

A woman was having an affair, and her husband came home and caught her and her boyfriend. Her husband was known to be a mean, rough man. The wife and boyfriend jumped into his convertible and took off from the island to Cortez Bridge. The husband jumped into his truck and followed. Once they got to the bridge, it started to rise. Knowing that the husband was coming up behind them and feeling like they had no choice, they tried to jump the bridge. They didn't make it, and both were decapitated. The shadows of two headless figures have been seen walking on the bridge.

There also was another gentleman named Jimmy, who was riding on the tailgate of a pickup truck and fell off when the driver went over a bump. He was run over and killed by the car behind them. He's reported to be seen walking the bridge at night too.

Joe's Eats and Sweets

Joe's Eat and Sweets has got the best handmade ice cream around. Opened some twenty years ago by Joe and his wife, JoAnn, the ice cream shop started up in the back of a surf shop, but it has now taken over the whole building.

Joe's wife passed away two years ago. Employees state that they hear voices but can't make the words out. They experience the feeling of being watched and see shadows. They believe that it's JoAnn, watching over the business. During an investigation there, we received two words. The first was *January*—Joe told us that this is the month his wife died. We then received the word *pendant*—again Joe told us that he bought his wife a special gift, a pendant, before she passed away.

Seemingly, JoAnn isn't the only spirit on the property. She is joined the spirit of a fisherman who died in the cottages that stood on the property before Joe's building was built. There is also a Spaniard from the 1500s there, but his spirit only responds to Spanish-speaking guests.

Beach House

Ed Chiles, son of the late governor of Florida Lawton Chiles, is well known for his innovative restaurant group. He bought the old Harbor House in 1993 and remodeled it into the beautiful, successful beachfront destination that it is today. The spectacular views of the Gulf of Mexico and the wonderful sunsets make the Beach House a place that can't be beat.

It is also known for having more than one hundred weddings on the beach per year, and one particular wedding comes to mind. In 2003, a bride was at the Beach House getting ready for her wedding when the employees received a call telling them that the groom wasn't going to make it. He had been killed in a car accident on the way to the ceremony. He is known to wander the beach at night around the beach house and has talked to us on our ghost walk. He's letting us know how sorry he is that he caused his girlfriend so much pain.

Curry House

In 1923, Henry Curry built an eighteen-room house with a large porch looking over the shoreline of Bradenton Beach. The home hosted many guests over the years and was later abandoned. One couple, Romaine and Glenn, purchased the house sometime in the '90s with the intention of restoring it.

At first, harmless little things began to happen. Their two dogs refused to enter the house and barked and howled all night outside. Then Romaine swore that she saw some antique dressers in the closet. When she went to look again, they were gone. Romaine became so uneasy in the house that she arranged for a séance. During the ritual, a female spirit is said to have appeared floating down the stairs. She was dressed in a navy blue traveling suit. She revealed herself as Estrella. The local historical society later confirmed that a woman with a Spanish name had possibly lived in the house, but she died before she could move in. She was known to break things that she didn't like.

Glenn grew tired of all the chaos and determined to learn more about her history. Apparently, Estrella had died in a shipwreck from Boston to Bradenton while on her way to marry her fiancé. Also on this ship was Captain Curry, who built the house.

Over the years, the house was so inhabited by spirits that no one could live there. Many hear scratching on the walls, and the faint fragrance of orange blossoms lingers inside and out. If you walked off the property, the scent disappeared.

A captain wearing seaman's clothing is seen on the beach smoking a Cuban cigar and whistling. Tenants were always seeing shadow people. A woman who drowned while out sailing has been seen walking with a young boy and his Dalmatian dog on stretch of beach by the house.

Above: Curry House. *From the* Bradenton Herald.

Left: Glen and Romaine Thomasson, owners of the Curry House. *From the* Bradenton Herald.

When I was doing research for our island ghost walk, the chief of the Bradenton Beach Police department told me that I had to make sure that the Curry House story was in it. The police answered a lot of calls to the Curry House and could not explain a thing about what was going on.

The house was torn down in 2004 due to the fact that no one entering would even consider buying it, and the owners could never get anyone to rent it. Activity is still happening today where the Curry House once stood. Tearing it down and building a condominium complex has not stopped the spirits.

GULF OF MEXICO

Out in the Gulf of Mexico, off Anna Maria Island, we've had three shipwrecks. The closest wreck is the SS *Regina*. In 1940, the *Regina*, a sugar barge built in 1904 in Belfast, sank off the coast during a storm. The remains are in about 20 feet of water, and for a long time, you could see it sticking out of the surf. It's just 150 feet or so off the beach, and the wreck is more than 200 feet long. The location is marked with a buoy. This is Florida's tenth underwater preserve and is known to be snorkeling heaven—diving among the ruins and the sea creatures that have made it their home.

In the tragic wreck, all but the cook and his dog survived. They are seen walking down the beach heading south at night. He disappears when he knows you have spotted him.

The USS *Narcissus*, a screw steamer, was launched in July 1863 as the *Mary Cook* out of New York. In September 1863 it was, purchased by the U.S. Navy. After surviving the Battle of Mobile Bay, it was sunk at its own mooring by an old planted mine in 1864. At the end of the Civil War, after lengthy repairs, it was on its way home when it was lost off Egmont Key, which is part of Anna Maria Island off the northern tip of the island.

In 1866, *Narcissus* and another vessel, *Althea*, were ordered to return to New York. Both vessels ran into a terribly violent storm off Tampa. The *Narcissus* sent up several flares, and the *Althea* responded but unfortunately received no answer to its messages. *Narcissus* had run aground on a sandbar traveling at full speed. The cold water coming into the hot boiler caused the ship to explode. After a two-day search, no survivors were found.

Scuba divers get chills going through the area and looking at all the history that is preserved underwater. It is said that boaters above the wreckage also get chills just being in the area and hear voices looming over the waves.

In the late 1700s, the *Sunshine*, a British ship, was heading north to Tampa during a storm when a ten-foot boat came alongside asking if it needed help. When the *Sunshine*'s captain replied yes, not knowing what was in store for them, he unwittingly permitted the hijackers to tow them right into the hands of the pirate Miguel and his crew. Miguel, a vicious man, killed everyone on board, including thirteen women and children. He was the main pirate in the area.

The British sent a ship to apprehend Miguel but never caught him even after several attempts. His fellow pirates, however, did find him and hanged him on the south end of Longboat Key for breaking the pirate code against murdering women and children. Anna Maria and Longboat where still one island at this time.

Shadow people are seen on the tip of island. We have made a lot of contact via K2 meters and voice box equipment used on the beach during our ghost tours, including a young girl that says she is fourteen years old and was on the *Sunshine*. A lot of spirits just passing through the area will stop and talk to us too.

Egmont Key

A small island of its own, Egmont Key is at the northern tip of Anna Maria Island. Spanish expeditions first sighted it in the 1500s, but evidence of Native Americans was found going back farther in time. The first recorded contact with the island was in 1757 by Don Francisco Maria Celi, an early explorer. In 1763, the second Earl of Egmont was John Perceval. At this time in history, Florida was under British rule, so he was able to name the island after himself.

At the time, Egmont Key was 50 percent bigger than it is today. Violent storms, erosion and climate changes have made it what it is today. Since there was no fresh water, and travel on and off the island was only by water, it is believed that Native Americans only using this island for hunting and fishing. It is only accessible by boat and today holds the ruins of more than seventy buildings, a working lighthouse and a cemetery.

The island became a line of defense for the Spanish, a base for Union soldiers and a prison camp for the Seminole Indians. The first lighthouse was built in 1848 on the western gulf. After the hurricanes of 1848 and 1852, it was so badly damaged that they moved it more inland and rebuilt

Right: The Egmont Key lighthouse. *Manatee County Library*.

Below: The Egmont Key cemetery. *Manatee County Library*.

it in 1857–58. It remains in service even today, guiding mariners through the channels.

In the beginning of the Civil War, Egmont was occupied by Confederate blockade-runners. And in the late 1860s, Union forces used Egmont to execute their Blockade of Confederate Ports. When the Union soldiers approached, George V. Vicker, the lighthouse keeper and a Confederate sympathizer, left the island, taking the very expensive beacon lens with him. He was never seen again. Egmont was also used as a refuge for Union sympathizers and as a military prison during the war.

Construction of Fort Dade started in 1898 with temporary gun batteries built to protect Tampa during the Spanish-American War. The Spanish never came. The fort had three hundred residents, brick streets, a small railroad, an electric plant and seventy buildings, a bowling alley and a movie theater were included. There was also a tennis court.

During World War I, Fort Dade was used as a training center for the National Guard Coast Artillery Units. In the early 1920s, it was deactivated, and on October 25, 1921, it was hit by a hurricane. It was decided that it was too costly to repair so it was deactivated. However, it was reactivated for World War II as a harbor patrol station.

In 1854, members of the Seminole nation were detained at the fort before being sent to reservations in Oklahoma and Arkansas. Several original natives never left the island and are buried in mass graves.

Teddy Roosevelt and the Rough Riders were stationed on the island for training before heading off to Cuba, where they fought in the Battle of San Juan. In 1923, the fort was disbanded and taken over by bootleggers and pirates. In 1930, out of frustration, the U.S. Coast Guard started a grass fire to smoke them out.

In 1974, the local government created a wildlife refuge that is still open to this day. You may feel a chill, hear a voice or see something out of the corner of your eye while visiting during daytime hours. Only the rangers on patrol are on the island in the darkest hours, left with the spirits roaming their land. They've reported hearing piercing screams and conversations that can't be made out. Sometimes they see the old lighthouse keeper walking around the lighthouse and hear someone whistling "Dixie."

One ranger reported hearing a door slamming shut over and over again. When he arrived to where the noise was coming from, all the doors were shut and locked. Others have reported seeing apparitions of Civil War–era spirits walking around and units of gray-clad soldiers all lined up, ready for roll call.

Some believe that the Native Americans buried in the mass grave are wandering the island, and others believe they could be Spanish soldiers who died on the island during the Spanish-American War. Either way, there is lot of spirit activity going on.

ELLENTON/GAMBLE PLANTATION

In 1870, Major George Patten and his wife, Mary, purchased the Gamble Plantation and named the area Ellenton after their daughter, Ellen. The antebellum mansion was home to Major Robert Gamble and the headquarters of an extensive sugar plantation. It is the only surviving plantation house in South Florida. The house has survived wars, hurricanes and Florida's heat and humidity.

When Mr. Gamble arrived, he started right in, directing his slave workforce in clearing the land for sugarcane and fields and constructing the buildings. During this time, they were also fighting off Seminole attacks. The Gamble Mansion was built in 1844, shortly after the Second Seminole War ended. By the time Gamble finished his renovation and the land was up and running, he was so much in debt that he was forced to sell the planation and his slaves. Ultimately, he lived at Ellenton for only twelve years.

By the time the Civil War started, the plantation was in the hands of Captain Archibald McNeill, one of the most successful blockade-runners of the Confederacy. He kept supplies moving throughout the states during the war.

In 1865, Confederate secretary of state Judah P. Benjamin took refuge at the plantation after the fall of the Confederacy, knowing that he would be a wanted man to the Union army. He hoped to stay there until he could find safe passage to England. McNeill took Benjamin in and then worked out a plan to get him through the blockade. With his help, Benjamin was safely able to escape to Nassau. He later went on to London to practice law and retired in 1883. He later died in Paris, never to return to America.

After the Civil War, the mansion fell into disuse. For a time, it was used to store fertilizer. By the 1920s, it sat empty, decaying away until the United Daughters of the Confederacy stepped in to restore the building and grounds. The organization donated the house and sixteen acres to the State of Florida.

Gamble Plantation postcard. *Manatee County Library*.

Back in the 1990s, a paranormal group did an investigation out there and found no activity, but staff and visitors report seeing shadows walking around the property, as well as hearing voices. Occasionally, they will discover that ordinary objects have been moved, although no staff will admit to having moved them. Lights go on and off. Staff will see rocking chairs start moving, and wardrobe drawers have fallen out right in front of them. Staff believe this to be the spirit of a woman that appears in a brown dress, as well as Mr. Benjamin himself. Perhaps he finally came back to America. There could be more than just those two spirits. Some feel the presence of hardworking slaves wandering throughout the buildings and property.

PALMETTO

The city of Palmetto was settled by, Samuel Sparks Lamb in 1868. When it officially became a city in 1897, he named it after his home state of South Carolina, the Palmetto State.

Water was what brought the first settlers to this area, and soon yachtsmen and shippers discovered the beauty of the mile-long Manatee River. When the railroad expansion finally came in 1902, the center of activity for the town shifted from the waterfront to closer to the railroad depot, which was located on 10th Street. Lamb envisioned his property divided into a village. Over the years, he donated land out for a cemetery, three churches, a public library, a park and a woman's club.

James Howze came to Manatee County in 1885 from Alabama. He was a captain in the Thirty-Second Regiment of the Confederate army. He opened a store west of Lamb's original house and shop on the river. In August 1888, a salesman from Tampa arrived on a steamer and called on Mr. Howze. The man was so ill that Howze took him to his uncle, Dr. Astonish. That afternoon, when the steamer made its trip back to Tampa, the man went with it. A few days later, Mr. Howze received word that the man died of yellow fever. A few days after that, Mrs. Howze and their children came down with yellow fever. The children survived, but Mrs. Howze did not. She was the first of many yellow fever victims in Manatee County.

On a quiet acre in west Palmetto lies a sporadic array of tombstones, barely legible from more than a century of exposure to the elements. Many original settlers of Palmetto are buried there. This cemetery is known for the "Yellow Fever Cemetery." It was opened in the middle 1800s and closed in

Palmetto. *Manatee County Library.*

1910, the year Mr. Lamb died of yellow fever. The cemetery holds forty-four markers, but there are many more unmarked graves.

When the yellow fever breakout reached its height, traffic coming into Bradenton came to a halt. No one was allowed in the city to keep the disease from spreading. Armed guards were posted to keep anyone from entering the city, and people caught sneaking in were shot. Some believed that the Spanish moss carried the disease and that it was highly contagious. Of course, it was really the mosquitos that were the carriers.

Sometimes the disease would leave sufferers in a deathlike, comatose state. Believed dead, their bodies were thrown into the pile of corpses waiting to be buried at the gravesite. Every so often, gravediggers were treated to the eerie sight of a hand reaching out from the mound of bodies in need of rescue. This became such a commonly feared occurrence that it created the trend of the bell at gravesites. Wealthy people would arrange to be buried in a single grave with a ring placed around their middle finger. The ring was attached to a chain connected to a bell aboveground. If that person woke up in the tomb, he or she could ring the bell to alert the living that someone was in need of rescue.

It would take about four men to dig up a grave in a few minutes, but still that wasn't always fast enough. Stories abound of would-be rescuers opening a coffin only to find the person's hands with ripped-out fingernails or skin completely torn down to the bone. People would panic and hyperventilated very quickly as they tried to tear their way out.

Spirits wander the cemetery grounds but don't leave the area. Footsteps are heard at times, but no one is there.

Norma Rae's Restaurant

Built in 1896, the first Beall's store was opened by R.M. Beall and his father, Augustus Beall, on Main Street in 1914. Frank's newspaper stand was in the alleyway next door. It was said that Frank's newspaper stand had an area in the back for adult material. Frank's moved across the street, and nowadays, you can only see the alleyway from the back alley behind the buildings. The alley now has a gate. Shadows are seen walking around behind the gate sometimes on.

Norma Rae's Restaurant is now at this location and seems to have activity from both Frank's and Beall's. The building is full of activity, from voices to eerie shadows and even a full-body apparition. The owner has seen a shadow figure walk across the kitchen multiple times. A lot of banging is audible, as though someone were getting ice from the ice machine when no one is there. There is a man there that sits at the counter asking for help during business hours. Several police officers and a waitress saw a man dressed in a dark suit standing by front door area, and just as they saw him and tried to approach, his figure just disappeared. Voices have been caught saying "Hello" and "Yes."

The restaurant is now closed.

Harllee House

Located on the Manatee River, the Harllee House was built in 1899 for Julius A. Lamb, one of the sons of the founder and mayor of Palmetto. The house was then purchased by J. Pope Harllee in 1919. It stayed in the Harllee family until 1991. J. Pope Harllee became a farmer, and in 1906, he formed Harllee Farms, which is still in operation today and provides the area with a variety of tomatoes.

The Harllee House has three floors, twenty major rooms and four bathrooms. The most notable features are the octagonal turret towers and the stately column porches.

A young couple bought the property in 1995 and began working to restore the handcrafted beauty of the house. Right away, supernatural things started happening. At times, early in the morning, the couple could hear someone cooking in the kitchen yet no one was ever found. The couple often heard footsteps echoing throughout the house. They believed this to be the spirit of Mrs. Harllee. While restoring the house, the new owners found a love letter Mrs. Harllee wrote to the house itself, extolling its beauty and comfort and expressing how much she enjoyed hosting guests. Perhaps she couldn't bring herself to leave her beloved home, even in death.

The couple has since given up on the restoration, sold the home and moved on, letting the spirits be.

Emerson Point

Emerson Point is located at the mouth of the Manatee River, where it meets lower Tampa Bay. This 365-acre preserve located at the tip of Snead Island has a long and rich history of human habitation going back thousands of

Emerson Preserve. *Author's collection.*

years. It is a favorite place for fishermen because of its protected water, sea grasses and fifteen miles of shoreline. There are a lot of hiking trails and an observation tower to take in the breathtaking view from sixty feet above the ground.

Walking the trails leads hikers to a thousand-year-old American Indian village. It's easy to imagine the sun gleaming off the shell mounds and smoke coming from the campfires, remnants from a culture that existed more than one thousand years ago.

The trail ends in a clearing. To the right is the Manatee River, and to the left is the largest Native American temple mound in Southwest Florida. It is the Portavant Temple Mound, with its 150-foot flat top. This temple also has subsidiary mounds, which are rare in the United States, and no one really knows what they were used for or their significance. As each leader died, the remains were allowed to decompose, and then they would burn his home and bones and rebuild a new leader's home on top. Walking around, you will notice the erosion that is happening to the mound from Mother Nature.

Imagine all the trees there gone. A lookout would have a clear view of the open waters in case someone was coming to attack. That is how it looked to them. Natives started building this in AD 800 and abandoned it in AD 1500. The mound is all made from fish bones, shells and pottery pieces. It is all covered in grass now and on the edge of it sit the remains of Robert

Stewart Griffith's house, built in 1866. A walkway takes you over the mound to see the remains of Robert's house. If you are walking down by the water close to where their home stood, you may encounter Robert and his wife. It seems that his wife went out to the water and started drowning. Robert went in to save her and drowned along with her.

Walking through the area, you will feel chills on the hottest days. This place can be pretty active at night. I would love to stand on the observation tower and watch the activity that goes on—from shadows moving around through the mounds and voices being heard. Sometimes it sounds like Native American chanting. The smell of the campfires burning and the sounds of Native Americans doing their normal daily chores are experienced. Even Native American full-body apparitions are seen at times.

They once allowed paranormal groups to go through but no longer do. It seems to upset the Native American spirits.

Skyway Cemetery

Skyway Cemetery is located on Highway 19 on the right-hand side of the road. It's a big cemetery and is the most common place in the area to be buried. The cemetery's paranormal activity is sometimes heightened at night. The left side seems to be the most active. People have reported seeing shadows walking around, hearing voices and experiencing very cold spots during the hot summer nights in Florida.

On one occasion, someone had a young woman make contact with the spirits. They reported that they sat there for an hour talking with her and had a very cold spot right next to them. When the cold spot went away, the young woman stopped talking to them.

FROM AN INTERVIEW WITH KIM AND BRANDON BASSETT, PARANORMAL ENTHUSIASTS
My wife and I went out to Skyway Cemetery to try out a new infrared camera. We also took digital recorders, K2 meters and a device that plays random radio station noise. It is believed that spirits can use the device to use their energy to manipulate the radio frequencies to say words. We walked around the cemetery for about an hour without picking anything up. At the end, we sat down, and within two minutes, we captured what sounded like male and female spirits were having, a conservation. First a female voice comes through the device saying, "Help...stop." Ten seconds later, a female

voice says, "Please…it's…it's," followed by a squeal noise. Then, sixteen seconds later on the digital recorder, you hear a male voice saying, "It's out of the woods now." Five seconds after that, a female's voice comes through the device saying a long drawn-out "Patiencccce." Five seconds after that, a man's voice is heard on the digital recorder saying, "Winwood's coming." We captured nothing for the next twenty minutes and left. It should be noted that this cemetery is surrounded by woods.

Skyway Bridge

In the 1970s and 1980s, multiple reports were made of a blond woman jumping from the southbound side of the Skyway Bridge. The police were called out to the site for every report, but after searching the bridge and water, nothing was ever found. In the 1970s, tollbooth collectors reported a blond woman jumping off the bridge. In the early 1980s, drivers claimed to have seen a blond female hitchhiker on the bridge. When picked up by motorists, she would disappear from their back seat. After the bridge was destroyed in an accident in 1980, she was never seen again.

Summit Venture hit the Skyway Bridge at 7:33 a.m. on May 9, 1980. *From the* Bradenton Herald.

On May 9, 1980, the original Skyway Bridge was hit by a 608-foot cargo ship named the *Summit Venture*. Harbor pilot John Lerro hit the bridge when a small squall came up from nowhere, causing blinding rains and winds over seventy miles per hour. When the sun broke through, it was too late for Lerro to do anything. The impact caused a 1,300-foot segment of the bridge to collapse. Six cars, a pickup truck and a Greyhound bus with twenty-two passengers and the driver went over, resulting in the deaths of thirty-five people. They fell 200 feet at sixty-seven miles per hour. The truck somehow hit the ship and then fell into the water. The driver of the truck was the only one who survived. John Lerro was haunted for the rest of his life. He died in 2002 at the age of fifty-nine.

This new bridge is used quite a lot, not by traffic but by those committing suicide. More than one hundred have succeeded, and more than that number have been stopped. There are emergency suicide hotline phones installed at the highest point of the bridge.

While fishing off the pier, which is the old bridge, people have seen the "ghost bus." It's seen traveling down the pier with the bus driver staring straight ahead and a woman in the back window dressed in black waving. It then falls into the water. Many claim to feel a breeze and smell gasoline as it passes them.

Sea Hut/Old Crab Trap Restaurant

Built in 1976, Old Crab Trap was a little thatched roof restaurant on the tip of Snead Island. Eight years after being built, it moved location to a bigger area. Lee Cline and his wife, Margaret, started the restaurant, which was handed down to their daughter, Donna, and their grandson, Jarrett.

The family and staff have believed for a long time that Mr. Al, who managed the restaurant until his death in the 1990s, haunted the building. Many different incidents have led them to believe something was there, and after an investigation was done, Mr. Al was found to be present. Via equipment and a voice box, he answered questions to state that he was there. The current manager will sometimes leave his favorite drink on the bar, and he has let her know that he enjoys it.

Stop by the Sea Hut for a bowl of its clam chowder and have a talk with Mr. Al. He's still watching over the place to this day, making sure that the restaurant is running smoothly. Mr. Al was in the navy, so you may be able to get a conversation going with him by bringing up service in the navy.

PARRISH

Parrish Cemetery

Alice Turner Berry inherited the grounds of Parrish Cemetery from her father, Major William Iredell Turner. After Alice's death in 1846, her heirs turned the land over to the trustees of the Parrish Cemetery.

The earliest headstone found in this cemetery belongs to Rose Lee Turner, who was born on February 22, 1876, and crossed over on October 21, 1876.

There are two roads leading into the cemetery. That's because this has a white section and a black section, once separated by a fence. Some of the old gravestones in the black section were hand-carved by family members.

While doing an investigation at the cemetery, our video camera caught footsteps coming toward the camera, which was sitting on a tripod; it was picked up and moved, then the footsteps walked away. Since there were only two of us out there and we were both together on the other side of the cemetery, we know it wasn't us moving the camera or the creating the sound of the footsteps.

Parrish Cemetery. *Author's collection.*

Shadows are seen peeking around tombstones, and voices are heard. You may sometimes see shadows go from tombstones to the tree line, and occasionally you will hear cows mooing in the background.

Rye Preserve

Rye Preserve is 145-acre preserve in Parrish. Known for its hiking trails, horse trails and kayaking, it has a little bit of everything for nature lovers. There are four trails that will lead you through four different ecosystems, with rare animals and plants. Within the preserve is a piece of Manatee County pioneer history: the Rye Cemetery. This is all that is left of the Rye community.

In 1889, Erasmus and Mary Rye moved to this area to establish a homestead. A small community grew up around the Rye homestead. At its peak in the early 1900s, Rye had seventy-two families living in this community, along with stores, a post office, a school and a sawmill. In 1910, the United States government dredged the Manatee River, opening it to steamships. Then cars and trains made it easier to travel. The steamship lines went under, and so did the community of Rye.

If you are brave enough, you can spend the night camping on the preserve. Stories have been told of hearing voices and seeing Confederate soldiers. I've been told by a few people that they hear a breath or sigh in their ear, but when they turn, no one is there. It's been said that there are Confederate soldiers buried there in unmarked graves. They were buried where they died, never making it back home to their families.

In the middle of a clearing, there is a well-maintained cemetery. It's a small cemetery that has a lot of children's graves. Back in the day, it was common for children to die young because of disease, accidents or birth defects. If you are out by the cemetery at night, it's been said that you can hear the voice of children and footsteps. Conversations are heard but you aren't able to make them out, and someone is heard breathing in your ear. Shadows are seen, even small ones peeking out from behind tombstones.

There is also a story about Lake Manatee. The lake sits about half a mile southeast of the official preserve property lines. While swimming, people feel human hands grabbing at their legs or grabbing their bathing suits and attempting to drag them underwater.

DUETTE

Established in 1888 with a post office that remained open until 1907, Duette is an incorporated community of Manatee County. It has the largest nature preserve in Manatee County, about twenty-one thousand acres in total. At one point, it was owned by the railroad, but nothing was ever done out in the area by the railroad management.

The community is named for a Canadian settler. Many Native Americans battles took place in this area. Numerous Confederate soldiers have walked this land. People in the community tell stories of the eerie things they've seen and heard that defy rational explanation. The tales encompass everything from cowboys on horseback to strangers seen standing by the doors of people's homes as they pull up in driveway—the spirit will vanish as soon as anyone approaches.

Bunker Hill Winery

The first time I went out to this area, I went to Bunker Hill Winery for its "Orb Walk." It has become my favorite place to go for peace, quiet and

Figure caught at Bunker Hill Winery. *Author's collection.*

the spirits. The winery is renowned for both its fantastic line of homemade wines and the spirits that roam the grounds. You won't be disappointed. Lenora and Larry Woodhaven, the owners of the winery who also conduct the Orb Walk, are wonderful people who will tell you about the history and activity that goes on there.

Bunker Hill Winery opened in 2010 as a twenty-three-acre winery and soon became known for being the greenest vineyard and winery in America. It is also certified as a wildlife habit. You may run across a 'possum, bobcat or even a wild boar. From the sixty-eight varieties of unfiltered wine to wine jams, jellies and preserves. I feel that Lenora and Larry were called to this little piece of heaven. They are the perfect people to own and live here. I'm not sure exactly what the land was used for before they owned it, but it was likely a private residence.

Lenora and Larry have had a number of uncanny experiences out at the winery themselves. Lenora would hear her name being called when no one was around, and Larry's tools would disappear and then reappear just where he left them. Tombstones erected for pets that have passed away have been totally moved from their spots. With all that activity, they decided that they wanted to share their story with anyone who wanted to hear about it.

A psychic woman who was visiting the Bunker Hill Winery asked Lenora and Larry if they knew that a spirit named Gerald was there. They didn't know anyone by that name but were informed later by the son of one the previous owners that when his father died, his ashes were spread out by the creek that runs through the back property. They were told that the father's name was Jerald.

The winery offers wine tastings and Orb Walks. The Paranormal Society of Bradenton, Florida, has done a lot of investigations out there, and the activity is amazing, from orb activity that follows you to the voice of a little girl saying, "I love you," as well as others talking. There is believed to be a portal out there, and I don't doubt it. A portal is an energy vortex that acts as a channel for unrelated spirits to travel to and from the physical realm.

At the guesthouse, we caught so much orb activity on camera. Some would actually come up to the camera, back up and then come back up to the camera. Guests staying there reported the presences of a woman and man in the guesthouse, but I believe there to be more. You frequently have the feeling of someone watching you or catch someone walking by out of the corner of your eye. Several guests have seen a man and a woman.

My personal experience there involved seeing a Confederate soldier walking toward me. It seemed like he was coming home from the war. He looked worn out, and his uniform was dirty. He looked directly at me and disappeared. What I remember the most was the uniform. I described it to Larry, a Civil War enthusiast, and he said he didn't know of any uniform that looked like that. I spent some time searching for that uniform jacket and finally found it. I gave a copy to Lenora and Larry. Larry was surprised to see that I had found the unique uniform because he didn't believe the uniform existed. Other people have caught the outline of the soldier in their photos.

There was a battle that went on at the property between the pioneers and Native Americans. This place is very special and gives you a feeling of calm. Not one spirit is negative in any way. They are very friendly spirits and really enjoy communicating with the living.

Like many wineries, Bunker Hill is frequently used as a venue for wedding ceremonies. The area where the wedding arch is located seems to be some sort of opening. While our DVR camera was focused on this area, we caught hundreds of orbs flying out from the middle of the arch that then followed me and my daughter to the area where there is a round table. We sat down, and it actually looked like it was snowing. Some will say it's just bugs, but it

Orb and mist caught at Bunker Hill Winery. *Author's collection.*

was January in Florida and a cold night, as you could see by the way we were dressed. We left the table area, and they followed us. When we returned to the table area, they returned with us. At one point on the camera, a huge bright orb came out from the arch, and that ended the activity for the night. If you get a chance, go on the winery's Orb Walk and see what happens to you. This is one amazing place.

DE SOTO NATIONAL MEMORIAL PARK

In 1539, conquistador Hernando de Soto's army of soldiers and nine ships landed in the Tampa Bay area. The ships carried 220 horses, priests, craftsmen, engineers, farmers and merchants. Some were even traveling with their families. They were met by the fierce resistance of Native Americans protecting their land. This was the beginning of the first extensive organized exploration by Europeans of the southern United States. De Soto was known to be a cruel man. He killed most of the Native Americans, took their food supplies and kept a few alive for slaves. He journeyed through Florida, Georgia, Mississippi, Alabama and Arkansas, killing and stealing all along the way. He took two male Native Americans as guides so they could speak to the tribe members they encountered. He was the first European known to cross the Mississippi River.

This expedition turned out to be a bad one for De Soto—starvation, disease and ambush attacks were killing off the people he had brought from Spain as well as his crew. This also turned out to be his last expedition. He was on a search for the City of Gold and a passage to China. The hardships were staggering, and they gave up on their search for the city. These trials caused a lot of the survivors to kill and eat their horses, all while struggling to make boats to escape via the Gulf of Mexico.

De Soto's armies were attacked after trying to force their way into a cabin occupied by Chief Tuskaloosa, a Mississippian leader. The Spaniards fought their way into the town and burned it to the ground. It's said that during the nine-hour fight, 200 Spaniards died and 150 were badly wounded and an estimated 2,000 to 6,000 native warriors were killed, making this the one of the bloodiest early battles in recorded North American history.

In May 1542, De Soto died of a fever on the banks of the Mississippi River. The true location is unknown, as his men wanted to conceal his

De Soto landing marker. *Author's collection.*

Huts at De Soto National Memorial. *Author's collection.*

death. According to some, De Soto's men hid his body in blankets and weighed it down with sand. They carried him out to the Mississippi River during the night and dumped him overboard.

The memorial park covers twenty-six acres and has three thousand feet of coastline, mostly thick mangrove swamps. There are hiking trails and a little town to show you how the community lived back then. Locals say that while walking the coastline at night, you may come across shadow people wandering around. Unknown voices are heard, their words indistinguishable. Up by the little town, things are known to move around to different areas, and a pot hanging over a fire may start swaying back and forth. Footsteps are heard. No one knows for sure whether it's the Spaniards or the Native Americans, but whoever it is still remains.

Park at the De Soto National Memorial. *Author's collection.*

Investigations and Legends

T he following stories are from investigations that our group has done or locals who don't want their names or locations to be divulged. Their stories are real and they want them told, but some are afraid of the nonbelievers.

Healthcare and Public Service

Blake Hospital

Located in West Bradenton off 59th Street West, Blake Hospital was built about forty years ago and is still in use today. Over the years, the building has been remodeled, updated and developed. During times of disruption, staff would report activity going on in the old delivery area. Some say it was stories made up by staff, and others say they witnessed weird things happening directly.

Staff reported hearing babies crying and footsteps and seeing glimpses of figures in white walking around. Others have said that, at times, you can see spirits wandering around the hospital, and patients have seen some of these spirits going by their door or stepping into their room and then disappearing. Seeing dark shadows wandering around is also common there.

Unnamed Nursing Home

At its request, this local nursing home asked to be left unnamed in this book (as it is still in business), but it was more than willing to share some of its ghost stories.

The staff at this nursing home, have a few stories to share. In room 118, staff report hearing noises coming from the room when no one was living there. They would go check on the noise and what caused it and were hit with very cold air upon entering. The air conditioning in the room was turned off, so it couldn't have been that. This happened three times in one night, and they could not figure out what was causing the noise or the coldness.

Two young women reported seeing a woman wearing a white coat. At the same time this happened, one of the old staff nurses passed away on the other side of the building. They believe that it was her returning to doing her job.

A patient named Mrs. Hope passed away. All night long, the lights in the hallway would turn on and off when someone walked down the hallway. Maybe this was her way of saying goodbye and "thank you."

In room 216, a patient died a rough death. From then on, staff, residents and guests have seem a very dark shadow lingering in the hallway. These sightings continue to this day.

In room 215, the resident reported daily that she would see a half of a woman, from head to waist, moving around in her room. She became sick, and no one could figure out what the cause was, so the doctors decided that she was depressed. This illness continued until someone came in and performed a traditional sage burning ceremony around her room to cleanse and quiet the spirit activity in her room. She came out of the illness right away and has been smiling since.

Three different residents, who stayed in room 107 at different times, all reported seeing children in the closet of the room. These residents did not know one another and had not talked among themselves about seeing the children.

In room 124, staff reported hearing noises and banging. No one was staying in the room. The only thing that was in the room was an old dresser that had been in room 117. The patient who was in room 117 passed away, and her dresser was moved to room 124. Staff believed that she was letting them know she wanted her dresser back in her room.

There are also reports from staff that they have seen a very dark shadow that walks the stairwells and is seen by the doors to the floors.

Police Substation on 10th Street and 10th Avenue

I've been told so many stories from police officers about this substation that it's amazing they want to go in that building at all. Some have told me they don't want to return to it because of the overwhelmingly dark feelings and strange happenings they've experienced there.

This property housed a restaurant at one time, but I'm not sure what was there before that. The county built a police substation after the restaurant was torn down, and it was used for several years for training classes, were held on the top floor, as well as processing and holding prisoners on the bottom floor.

At one point, an officer was checking in a prisoner to the officer on duty. All three heard a noise and turned to see a black mass traveling toward them. It scared them so much that the prisoner asked to be taken somewhere else, and that police officer no longer enters the building. The officer on duty was accustomed to these things happening, so he just shrugged it off—that's not to say he enjoyed being there when things like that happened though.

Now that the building is hardly used, officers in the building alone will heard footsteps, doors opening and shutting and talking coming from different parts of the building. An extensive check of the building from top to bottom and the parking lot always confirms that the officer is the only one there. No one has figured out who is causing the disturbance and why, but it does continue today. They can never find any reason for the unexplained noises.

HAUNTED HOMES

Old House in Bradenton

There is a particular old house near downtown Bradenton that is more than one hundred years old. It was built for physically and mentally handicapped children. At that time, parents were known to just drop off their children at the property and never come back, as they didn't know how to take care of them.

The treatment to "cure" the children was often electric shock and ice bath treatments. These are definitely cruel procedures by today's standards, but back in the day, they didn't know that mental and physical illnesses like these children had couldn't be cured.

This is now a private residential home, and the owners will hear a little girl walking through the house crying for her "momma or grandma." She will walk up and down the stairs and the halls at night. We found out that her name was Pamela, and she let us know that her parents dropped her off there and never came back. She died from coughing. We figure she either caught pneumonia or drowned in an ice bath.

One of our investigators sat down with Pamela and spent an hour telling her to go into the light to find her momma and grandma. Since then, she has not been heard again in the house or made any contact with us.

A Local House

I will have to keep this location unknown at the owner's request, but I have permissions to share her story. The house was built in the 1970s and is like any 1,200-square-foot three-bedroom home. The owner has sadly lost two husbands in the house. Both died in the master bedroom area, and both died from heart issues.

She told me that she could be sitting in her favorite chair watching TV and would see out of the corner of her eye a shadow walk by or have the feeling of someone gently touching her from behind. We did an investigation of the house and found that both her husbands are there and are watching over her. We did catch a shadow and an EVP saying "I love you," which made her feel more comfortable in her home. She says the activity continues still today, but she is pleased knowing that they are there with her.

Evil in Bayshore Gardens

A couple bought and moved into a house in the Bayshore Gardens area of Bradenton. They felt that something wasn't right with the house from day one and were ready to move out before the first month was up. They were hearing voices and footsteps and had an overall feeling of being watched. The master bedroom closet seemed to be the center of the activity.

Every night at about 2:00 a.m., the couple would hear voices and music playing on a radio. Footsteps were audible going back and forth in the hallway, like someone was moving from one bedroom to the other. Strange shadows lurked in the corners of their vision. The family dog had started acting differently, always looking up and barking at something that couldn't be seen.

They called us in to see if we could help. As soon as we entered the house, I got goosebumps and felt all the hair on my body stand up. While checking out the rooms for anything electrical that could be causing high EMF reactions, we entered the one unused bedroom. A strong tingling feeling permeated the room. We left an EDI in there to see if it would let us know if anything was there.

Upon entering the master bedroom, it was like we were hit with a shock of electricity. The closer we got to the source, the stronger the feeling became. It got so bad at one point that one of the investigators had to hand off his equipment to another person and leave the room. He compared it to the feeling you get when your leg falls asleep and it starts to wake up.

After making contact with several spirits, we became concerned, as at one point the spirit answering on the voice box was telling us it was evil. After going through the evidence, we contacted Shaman Jeff Wheeler and Dawn Collins, owners of the Village Mystic store in the Village of the Arts in Bradenton, and asked them to join us on a return visit. We wanted Shaman Jeff to come and see what he felt. Being a shaman, he has access to the spirit world of both good and evil, and he is able to have some influence on the spirits. This takes a lifetime of training. Shaman Jeff typically walks around outside to get the feel of the property, but upon his arrival here, he said that they were immediately calling him inside.

Before Shaman Jeff and Dawn arrived, we asked the spirits if they knew what a shaman is and what he does. We received very strong "Yes" answers. When we asked if they were afraid of the shaman and what he was going to do, they answered "No."

When Shaman Jeff entered the house, he was immediately drawn to the master bedroom and the closet. Upon entering the bedroom and opening one side of the closet door, we could see shadows. After talking to the spirits, he found a portal in their closet. At one point, Shaman Jeff felt something touch the bottom of his leg, and we caught a voice saying, "Do you feel." I said, "That was strange," and we received an answer: "That was for you." At one point, a voice asked Shaman Jeff if he could "bring me back from the dead." Jeff then closed the opening, and the air in the room changed. It lifted and became lighter. But then we found out that there were a few others there that didn't want to leave.

There was a very strong, angry male spirit (named Edward) that we believe was the one telling us he was evil, as well as a female named Amber that felt she was being kept there by the man. Edward did curse a few times and fought against leaving the house. However, the female spirit, named Amber, was more than happy to join Shaman Jeff and leave with him. We caught on video an orb shooting into Shaman Jeff as he asked her to leave with him. We also caught on video the EDI we placed in the other bedroom going off when no one was in room. An EDI measures the EMF in the room, goes off from vibration and measures temperature changes. All three things were going off with no one in the room. You are later able to see a timeline graph to see when these events happened.

Shaman Jeff felt that Edward would leave shortly after Jeff left with the female spirit. At last check, Edward was still at the house, but he's not causing any more problems and the noise from the closet has stopped. There is another house in the area that has reported activity. A man with a top hat is seen walking around, and a woman is often seen hanging from the light fixture she hanged herself from. It seems to be a pretty active area.

Myakka House

We were called to a house. The present owner thought that it was haunted. The house was built in the early 2000s by a real estate agent and her husband, but as soon as they finished the house, they lost it in foreclosure. The second owner also lost the house to foreclosure a few years later. The current owner is also in foreclosure. It seems that no one can keep the house. It's said by the current owner that a lot of negativity was felt in house and that it caused problems so bad that the couple got divorced.

After the husband moved out, things began to happen. Shadows were seen, voices were heard and the younger children would no longer want to sleep in their rooms. At times, they would see the blinds in their house move on their own.

Upon our arrival at the site, two of us were drawn to the donkey field out back (so named, by us, because there were two donkeys in the field with us). After setting up our equipment throughout the property and house, three of us decided to go out to the field. Walking around the donkey piles, we ended up in the middle of the field when the activity started. We were getting direct answers to questions. A woman's voice was asking for "help," a team member was scratched on his back and we could feel cold air around us even though it was the middle of a hot, humid Florida summer night. It was cold enough to give you goosebumps.

Inside the house, a few team members were in the master bedroom, and the name "Kenneth" came through on the voice box. One of the investigators in the room was named Kenny. In one of the kids' bedrooms, three investigators had a feeling overcome them that made them feel ill; they had to leave the room. This was the bedroom for two small children who refused to sleep there after witnessing ghostly activity.

After we went through our evidence and did some research of the area, we found that it was old Native American land, and burial grounds were possibly located either on the property or nearby. It made us wonder if a contractor might have found some burial grounds when they were building the house and just covered it up to avoid the challenges that come with unearthing a historic site.

We returned to tell the owner that it wasn't the house—it was the property. While we were there, we went out to the field again and got more activity. Whoever or whatever remains on the property, they are upset and don't want anyone or anything disrupting them. I don't know if the last owner also lost the house or if she was able to sell. Good luck to whoever buys this property.

SHOPS AND RESTAURANTS

McCabe's Irish Bar

McCabe's Irish Bar is located on Old Main Street in downtown Bradenton. This building was once the very first Beall's store opened in Florida, but it was not called Beall's at the time. While renovations were taking place for McCabe's in 2006, the owners were cleaning out the crawl spaces under the floor when they came across two paintings. One was of two girls, and the other was of a woman.

Rumor has it that the woman painted the picture of two little girls whom she would see playing together. One day, she offered the girls a cookie, and the girls later died. She then painted a self-portrait before committing suicide. They have the picture of the woman hanging in the bar today. If you walk back to the ATM and look up through the slats you will see her.

It's also said that, at times, a bottle of alcohol will come off the bar and fall to the floor. Personally, I think that's spirits wasting spirits.

Tattoo Studio

The owners of a tattoo studio located on Old Main Street's south side have told me for the past four years that its property once served as a mortuary. Previous record searches have not confirmed this; however, before it was Classic Ink, the building was an art studio, and the woman who owned it lived above and ran the studio. She passed away, and when Classic Ink opened, the staff reported a cold wind rush through and footsteps pacing back and forth when they were closing up.

This continued for a while, and then they thought it was the artist who had once occupied the studio. So, they started to let her know that the studio was theirs while they were open and hers when it was closed. Since then, she has been happy with those arrangements and no longer paces back and forth or bothers the employees when they are closing up. She does, however, let them know she's still around.

As far as it being a mortuary, who knows? Perhaps the building was once used as an undocumented site to help with unreported injuries or illegal procedures done on women. Some history can't be found in the official records.

The Baker's Widow

A local baker, known to many, passed away unexpectedly at an early age and left his wife to continue on with the business. She had helped him for more than thirty years as the cake maker, while he made all the pastry and bread doughs. She assisted with the finishing of the pastries, but he was the one who really did the main baking.

After his death, his wife was trying to get back into the swing of things. Everyone's favorite was his Philly-style sandwiches, and what made them great were his special hoagie rolls. She was having a hard time trying to work with some of the recipes that were discovered in his huge collection of handwritten formulas. After several attempts at making rolls from different recipes that were not correct, she became frustrated. She decided to call us in, knowing that we could help contact him.

We set up our equipment in his home workshop and started running the SCD-2 voice box. Right away, the baker started talking. He recognized my husband, Ron, by saying "stovepipe hat," part of his garb he wears for our ghost walk and which was familiar to him. We told him we needed the recipe for the famous rolls or the sandwiches couldn't be made. You could hear female laughter in the background, and then we heard a male voice say, "She can do it." We believe this was his previously departed sister's, who also worked in the bakery. When we asked which was the correct recipe, he said, "page twelve." What page twelve? He told us, "The old gray book." Well, his wife pulled out several cookbooks, and there was an old gray composition notebook. Sure enough, there was a recipe for what she thought was the right one. In the following days, she tried the recipe but found that it *wasn't* the right one. When putting the cookbook back, she came across an even older gray ledger, and there was the correct recipe on page twelve. As she was making it, she said that she felt her husband's hands helping her make the hoagie rolls each step throughout the baking processes.

Also during this investigation, his wife got so excited when he said that about the old gray cookbook that she remembered that she promised to pour his favorite drink, and as she went to get it the SCD-2 said, "scotch and hoagies." She went to get his drink in his favorite glass.

As she was carrying it to his workshop where we were at, we asked if "he knew what she had," and very clearly you could hear him say, "it's a glass." We set it on his workbench, and he said, "Thank you." He also said what we all thought was "retire," making us think that he wanted his wife to retire. A few weeks later, though, she awoke to a fire in their home workshop, which caused her to relocate.

She is still continuing the family baking traditions and says that he is there helping her whenever she calls him.

The Old Painter

I've been told a story about a painter from back in the 1980s who would go from event to event around the area and have the creepiest-looking paintings of people. When looking at them, you would feel like they were staring at you no matter where you stood. You'd look up and their eyes would be on you, always. It was said that this painter would paint someone's picture, and then he or she would die after he finished the picture. It makes you wonder if he trapped their souls in the paintings. He hasn't been seen around in a long time—I wonder if he painted himself?

DE SOTO COUNTY

D e Soto County is on the east border side of Manatee County. It covers 639 square miles and was founded in 1887. It was named for Hernando de Soto, but since the name "Hernando" was taken by another county, they went with De Soto.

ARCADIA

Arcadia was known for its rough living. Back in the late 1800s, it was known as a wild and wide-open cow town. This was a lawless area. In 1870, the Barber-Mizell Range Wars broke out and spilled into the streets, claiming nine lives within three months. The feud between the two families started on February 21 when Sheriff Mizell had to follow up on a complaint with the Barber cattle operation. The Barbers killed the sheriff, and this started the war between the two families. One historian wrote that as many as fifty fights per day took place, and one fight caused the deaths of four men. On Thanksgiving Day 1905, the town burned down, and help came from everywhere to rebuild. The cause of the fire is unknown. But no matter what this town does, it always remains host to a number of spirits, perhaps even more than famously haunted cities like Key West or St. Augustine.

Arcadia Opera House

Arcadia Opera House was built in 1906, making it one of the first buildings constructed after the fire that destroyed most of the downtown area. It was used for plays, musical acts, political rallies and church functions. A screen was added when motion pictures came into prominence, and then movies were shown on a regular basis. It stopped being used in the 1940s. It is now home to shops on the bottom floor and an antiques mall and museum on the top floor.

It's commonly used by paranormal groups for investigations. The current owners rent out the building and allow you to investigate. It is said to have a lot of activity.

When we did an investigation there, we found a little girl looking at us from a window upstairs. We went to the room and got some activity on our meters letting us know that she was still in the room. We don't know her name, but it is said that she jumped from the second-floor window for reasons unknown.

On the stage is an antique horse-drawn hearse that the owner likes to display. Behind the hearse is a noose that is known to move on its own—it's said by the owner that a man is known to have hanged himself with it. I have not been unable to find out who the man was or why he hanged himself. A lot of banging goes on, as if someone is moving things, but no one is around. Footsteps are heard throughout the place, and a shadow figure is seen walking on the stage.

I was told by Millie Mierkiewicz, a guest at the opera house, that when she and her friend Rachel Douzykowski were there and it was getting near to closing time, they were about to leave the stage area near the hearse and the hanging noose. Rachel was standing by one end of the hearse, trying to find something in her purse, while Millie was on the other end about to walk over to Rachel. Right between them, a headboard was pushed with a great force down onto the stage floor, almost landing on top of Millie. It had fallen with such force that the owner, who had been elsewhere at the time, came running at the noise, thinking that he'd heard a gunshot. Millie feels that it was a spirit telling them to leave, as it was closing time and they were the last ones in the building. The owner did place the headboard back from where it fell and tried to make it fall again by jumping on the stage at different places, but it never even slipped a little. The owner told Millie that stuff like this happens all the time. Millie does plan on going back again, but she'll take a digital recording to see if she can get someone to answer why the board really moved and almost hit her.

Above: Arcadia Opera House stage. *Author's collection.*

Right: The Arcadia Opera House window from which a little girl jumped, it is said. *Author's collection.*

Old Blue House

There is an old blue house in Arcadia and is said to have been owned by a family in the early 1800s. The family was murdered, and the house was set on fire and burned to the ground. In the 1900s, when a new house was built on this spot, strange things began to occur. People saw the spirits walking around, still inhabiting the house built on top of their fiery graves.

The Hanging Tree

A tree stands on the outskirts of town that was used for the town hangings back in the 1800 and early 1900s. A very long history of hangings is present here. From murderers to runaway slaves, they all were hanged from that tree. It's reported that sometimes you will see a noose swinging in the tree or even a body hanging. Spirits are spotted walking around the area.

CARLSTROM FIELD

Carlstrom Field was opened in 1917 for training for army pilots to prepare for World War I. It had a total of ninety buildings on the property. In 1922, it was placed on inactive status, and all the buildings had been sold and removed by 1926.

A new facility was built on the same land in 1941 to prepare and train for World War II. Its last cadet graduated in 1945. When the facility closed after that, it left twenty-two empty buildings on the property, which had seen the loss of twenty-three men who crashed during training.

In 1958, the field became G. Pierce Wood Mental Hospital. Rumors of questionable healthcare practices surrounded the facility. Living conditions were terrible, and it acquired a reputation as a place of physical abuse and gruesome accidents. Three deaths were reported during the time it served as an institution. One was a patient left too long in a hot bath, which was one of their treatments to calm and control the patients. The bath cooled, and the man ultimately died of hypothermia.

Another patient cut both of his hands off with a table saw. Whether it was an accident or not, no one knows. The last death was a twenty-one-year-old man who died the day after being admitted. Investigators found toxic levels of medication in his blood. No one can account for how he was able to take such a deadly dose. The hospital was closed in 2002, and the living patients who remained were transferred to other hospitals or released into a normal life. For a time, the building housed sex offenders who had completed their sentence but were not ready to be released.

From 2007 to 2011, it became the De Soto County Juvenile Correctional Institute. It was considered a hard place to be sent to. Inmates were fed food that wasn't fit for human consumption. Some juveniles were beaten so badly by prison guards that they needed medical attention but weren't allowed the care. These practices led to infections, incorrectly healed bones and sometimes death. Former staff and children in the institute who wished to remain anonymous reported that conditions were horrible. It was permanently closed in 2011.

Most of the buildings still stand, and the property is for sale through the state. The state did open a driving school on some of the property for racecar training.

The twenty-three pilots who died during training at the early military training school are buried in the local cemetery. They are said to be seen wandering around the cemetery at night. There are reports of hearing screaming coming from the old buildings. Shadows are reported walking around the property, and visitors report a feeling of being watched. Some say that they experienced a very uncomfortable feeling just being on the property but, at the same time, felt like they were being called to go into the buildings.

There is not any good energy on that property due to the cruel treatment at the hospital and the correctional institute. Spirits will push, scratch and yell in your ear to scare you. Visitors are not allowed on the property. No trespassing signs are posted everywhere, and violators can be arrested for going on the property. I would follow the law. Plus, the spirits don't want you there and will make sure you know that and make you leave in some way.

Oak Ridge Cemetery

Oak Ridge Cemetery is the final resting place of the twenty-three pilots who died during training at Carlstrom Field. It is also the final resting place of five children of James and Annie Richardson. Annie is also there buried with her children. On October 25, 1967, all seven of the Richardsons became violently ill after eating lunch. Within twenty-four hours, all the children and

Annie were dead. Their food had been laced with pesticide. Both parents worked, and the children were in the care of their next-door neighbor, Bessie Reese. She served all the children a lunch prepared earlier that day by their mom: beans and rice and hog cheese.

Mr. Richardson was arrested for their murders and tried and convicted based on flimsy evidence. Decades later, he was freed when Bessie Reese confessed on her deathbed. She had been jealous of the happy family. It turns out that during the time of the murders, Reese was on parole for poisoning her ex-husband as well.

The spirits of the children are seen throughout the cemetery, and there are also mysterious lights seen on a place called "Goat Hill" that locals believe to be the spirits of the children.

PORT CHARLOTTE

Restlawn Cemetery

The very first house in Port Charlotte was built on this property. It is presumed to be the homestead of a farmer and is adjacent to the cemetery. It seems that at some point, the farmer, becoming discouraged, lost his mind and murdered his wife. The house was condemned by the county but is still standing today.

People hear voices and conversations between the spirits that can't be made out by the human ear. Shadows are seen wandering in the cemetery, and once in a while, people hear a scream. Could that be the scream of the farmer's wife? The neighborhood has also been bothered for years by the sound of huge swarms of bees, but there are no bees to be found in the area.

If you are thinking about doing some investigating there, *don't*. The cemetery has made an agreement with the families of loved ones buried there that no paranormal investigating is to be allowed, and that request needs to be honored out of respect.

Outside Arcadia is the ghost town of Pine Level. All that is left is the church and the Pine Level Cemetery, which happens to be in the middle of a cow pasture. An eerie feeling permeates the air out there, like you are being watched. But then it could be the cows.

Pine Level was known to be the largest and only town founded in De Soto County back in the 1850s. It had a courthouse, a jail, two churches, salons, stores and warehouses. It was known to be a great hideout for local gangsters. One gang that was known well around there was the Sarasota Gang, as its headquarters was in the town of Pine Level. In 1855, the gang members were arrested for a robbery, and by the time they went to trial, only nine members remained in the jail. The rest had escaped. The old jail was so poorly constructed that it was easy to escape from. The floors were also made of straw, which caused a lot of flea and lice problems. All nine of the men went on trial but were acquitted of the robbery.

The church that is still standing in what is left of the town today was also known to have had straw floors, causing more health problems.

GLADES COUNTY

LAKE OKEECHOBEE

Lake Okeechobee covers 730 square miles and stretches throughout five counties. It is the second-largest freshwater lake in the United States.

The area was first settled by the Calusa Native Americans before 1545. In the 1800s, Seminoles settled here, and there were a few battles fought on this land. The area is known to have some dark secrets. Two mass graves exist in this area. One was for victims of hurricanes and destructive storms who were buried on land. The other is in the lake, where thousands of bodies of unknown origin have been buried. Even today, researchers don't know whom these bodies belong to. There are tales of lake monsters, dinosaurs and ghosts by the hundreds. The burials happened so long ago that stories were likely only passed down through oral tradition.

In 1800s, the pioneers of Florida began to settle in this area, and they were disturbed to see human remains in the shallow parts of the water. Fishermen reported catching skulls instead of fish. In the early 1900s, a surveyor was clearing some land on Grassy Island and found fifty human skeletons under a few inches of sand. Grassy Island is not a natural island. It is lake bottom that has been exposed from water levels being lowered by drainage canals.

It was such a common sight to find these remains that in 1918 water levels dropped so low that it looked like a huge pumpkin patch. There are thousands of remains sitting on the bottom of this lake, but they aren't generally visible today due to the change in the flow and drain-off of the water. Yet even today, some people report seeing shadowy bodies floating atop the water.

At first, people thought this mass grave dated from the Seminole Wars, but only thirty people from this area died then. Perhaps the remains are from the hurricanes in 1926 and 1928, when more than two thousand people died? But all of those have been accounted for and are buried in a mass grave at Port Mayaca Cemetery.

Is it an ancient culture? Where are all their artifacts? All that is found are bodies. Some people have even theorized that they might be refugees from the city of Atlantis or even aliens from outer space.

According to legend, in February 1841, two hundred Seminoles, rather than be captured by invading explorers, sliced their own throats and jumped into the water, where their bodies disappeared beneath the waves. The story goes that a medicine man put a hex on the area that has become the known as the "Curse of the Everglades." Some consider the invention of this legend a mere marketing ploy.

Perhaps as a result of the curse, two plane crashes have occurred in that area: Flight 401 in 1972 and Flight 592 in 1996 (in which all on board died). Flight 401 crashed on December 29, 1972, causing 101 deaths out of 163 people on the plane. A burned-out landing gear light distracted the crew, which caused no one to see that the autopilot had been disconnected. As a result, the airplane lost altitude, could not recover and crashed into the Everglades swamps at more than two hundred miles per hour. It was the first crash of a wide-body aircraft and the second-deadliest commercial airplane crash at the time.

Shortly after the crash, members of the crew who had died began to appear on other planes. Captain Bob Loft was seen in the cockpits, the galley and standing in the aisles. At one point, a woman saw an ashen-looking man sitting in a seat on the plane. She was so worried about him that she called for a crew member to check on him. The man vanished right before the eyes of the crew member and others nearby. The woman who first saw him became so distressed that they had to restrain her. She finally calmed down and was shown pictures of the crew that died, and she picked out the photo of Don Repo, the flight engineer from Flight 401.

Bob Loft was also spotted wandering around a plane's undercarriage. He even spoke to the ground crew, telling them that no checks needed to be done, as he had done them all. The pilot of this flight was so unnerved that he canceled the flight.

Don Repo was known to be the more active spirit though. He was seen working on an oven on a plane, and on another flight, the pilot heard knocking coming from beneath the cockpit. He opened the compartment door and was surprised to come face to face with Don Repo. Surprise turned to horror when Repo disappeared in front of his eyes. After checking out the plane, a problem was found with the plane that could have caused a horrible crash. It was also discovered that parts from Flight 401 had been recovered for use on other planes. Once these parts were removed, the activity stopped.

Flight 592 crashed eleven minutes after takeoff from Miami as a result of a fire in the cargo compartment due to improperly stored cargo. All 110 people died on this flight. Witnesses in the air said it looked like what happens when you shoot a bullet into the ground. When it hit the ground, the plane was pulverized. Water and dirt flew up more than one hundred feet in the air, like a mushroom cloud. Some body parts were never recovered, and people say that they still can see passengers walking through the water of the Everglades. Others have heard cries for help, leading them to believe that both crashes have spirits wandering around in the Everglades.

Lake Okeechobee not only has spirits that wander around, but it is also said to have lost treasure and monsters. People have reported some kind of dinosaur creature seen in the area. Rumor has it that the location where the Okeechobee campground sits now was once used by a cult for satanic rituals. Some campers report feeling ill while in this area or will suffer from chronic nightmares. Some campers have woken up in the middle of the night suddenly with the ability to speak in tongues. More emotionally vulnerable people should avoiding camp at this location, for such a person may be at greater risk for becoming possessed by a demonic spirit.

The spirit of a young man walks around the water of the lake. Witnesses report that at one point during his walk, he will suddenly stop, and his head is sliced off his body. He is believed to be the spirit of a young man who died in a horrific boating accident.

So, if you are ever out there, pay attention to your surroundings. You never know what you will see or hear or feel at Lake Okeechobee.

OTHER GLADES COUNTY GHOSTS

Glades County's ghosts aren't just limited to the campgrounds. There is also a ghost seen along Highway 80. There is a dam there where it is said a man was robbed and murdered, and his body was dragged down into the water. He will appear in front of you, but it is a very quick look—just a glimpse of him letting you know that he's still there.

There also is a story of the bridge that goes over 2nd Street in Belle Glade. Over the years, kids would dare one another to balance on the handlebar railings of the bridge. It's said that one kid fell off and hit his head on the rocks, killing him. He is seen walking the handlebars of the bridge today. But if he notices you spotting him, he disappears.

On October 12, 1994, it was reported that a few visitors were sitting on the edge of the lake by the rim canal. They started to see a bright light in the sky. Thinking that it was a helicopter with a searchlight on it, they continued to watch it. As they continued to watch it, they saw it wasn't a plane or a helicopter. It was moving too fast and quietly for it to be either of those. They noticed that it came out from the trees, a disc-shaped object coming toward them. It flew over them a few times, and they reported a loss of time while this was going on.

HARDEE COUNTY

HARDEE COUNTY ORIGINS

The settlement of Hardee County started in April 1849, when the Kennedy-Darling Indian Post opened on Paynes Creek. In July 1849, an attack by Native Americans ended with two store clerks dead: George Payne and Dempsey Whidden. William McCullough and his wife, Nancy, were wounded. The survivors then set fire to the building and burned it down to the ground.

Fort Chokonikla, which mean's "burnt house," was built in October 1849 half a mile from the old trading post. The threat of war was all around, but the soldiers found that malaria and other illness were their real enemies. In July 1850, the fort was abandoned. In 1854, what is Hardee County today was opened for settlement. Immigration was slow due to the Civil War and the Native American wars. Between 1855 and 1858, Fort Green and Fort Hartsuff were established. During the Civil War, the Cracker farmers and cattlemen wanted no part of the conflict. However, some did own slaves.

The arrival of the Florida Southern Railway in 1886 brought a boom to Bowling Green and Wauchula. After settlement started to slow, Wauchula became the largest town in the county. The county now has a few stories of spirits at the Hardee Prison and Popash School and a few others wandering the streets of Hardee County.

Local legend tells of a ghost mailman seen walking around still delivering mail on foggy mornings, but he disappears as soon as you try to talk to him. Ghost lights can be seen on Heard Bridge Road, Beareah Road and County Line Road in Frostproof. If you sit in your car, you will see the lights approach.

In Avon Park, Florida, there was a lake called Lake Arcola. No one knows why it dried up more than forty years ago, but people report seeing a barefoot woman fishing in the area where the lake used to be. Some believe that she is the spirit of someone who died in the lake decades before.

Hardee Prison

Hardee Correctional Institution in, Bowling Green opened in 1991 to house adult males and has a maximum capacity of 1,541 prisoners, housing more than 1,000 criminals today. Some of the roughest men—murderers, rapists and thieves—are serving time in Hardee.

These are groups of men whom the average person would be afraid to be locked in with, but some of these men are afraid of being in that prison for reasons other than the violent crimes committed by their fellow inmates. Prisoners and staff have reported hearing footsteps and voices when no one is there. Some see apparitions at their cell doors, staring at them, and are terrified knowing that they are trapped and have nowhere to run.

No one knows who these spirits are, but maybe they are the dark spirits of those who lost their minds, coming back to take a few more souls with them. Some prisoners have lost their own minds in there and have been sent to mental institutions. Most hope that they get out of there alive and sane.

POPASH SCHOOL

Popash School was built in 1898. The Popash community was established in the 1850s and was a cattle farming town. In 1886, the future of the railroad held great promise for the town. Unfortunately, the town was passed over for Zolfo Springs. Popash then became a ghost town except for the school.

In 1912, a brick building was built for a new school, which remained open until 1948. Rumor has it that the original old wooden school burned to the ground, killing a few children, but I haven't found any proof of that. Since the school closed in 1948, it has sat empty and dilapidated.

Some people have claimed to hear children's voices inside the school, and sometimes the school bell has been heard ringing. Some have found children's handprints in the dust on window ledges. People are said to be seen staring out the windows at passersby, giving the area an all-around uncomfortable feeling.

Because of the condition of the building and trespassers, the structure was demolished in 2008. The activity stopped when the building was torn down.

BLOODY BUCKET ROAD

In the town of Wauchula, there is a road that dates back more than one hundred years. It is known as "Bloody Bucket Road." That's not the real name of the road, but it's the nickname that has stuck with this road for the last century or so. Driving down the road leads to a bridge that goes across a small waterway where the locals say the water has run red with blood.

The road's nickname comes from a local legend. Two freed slaves, a husband and wife, settled in Wauchula right after the Civil War. She was a midwife and became concerned that people were having too many children. She had never gotten over the heartrending tragedy of her own children being taken away when she was a slave. So, as a midwife, she started doing horrible things to the babies. She began suffocating and killing the babies she delivered and took their little bodies down to bury them on the banks of the river.

With so many babies dying in her care, townspeople stopped using her services, and her mental state deteriorated further. As the story goes, she was haunted by the souls of the babies and would find buckets of blood around her home. She would sit in a rocking chair out in her yard as the buckets would fill up with blood, and then she would carry the buckets down to the river and dump them. During one trip, she fell in the river and drowned. They said that the river ran red with blood for days.

Some still say that on a full moon, the river runs red and you can hear babies crying, the sound of someone falling off the bridge and the splash of water. Some say this is not a true story. The only way to prove it to yourself is to go there on a full moon and see what happens.

SEBRING

Harder Hall

Built in the 1920s, legend has it that the owner of this building died under strange circumstances on the property. People have been seen spirits roaming the courtyard and peeking out of the windows. It is currently abandoned, and trespassers are prosecuted.

Central Fire Station in Sebring

In 1912, the founder of Sebring, George Sebring, bought two two-wheel charts and eight hundred feet of hose. He donated them to the city, and the Central Fire Station was built in 1913 at the end of East Center Street. It was relocated to Mango Street in 1922. Forrest Howard, the fire chief from the 1930s and 1940s, is seen wandering the halls and in the bunk area by the firemen stationed there. Sometimes the scent of his favorite cigars lingers in the air.

PELICAN ALLEY RESTAURANT

Located at the base of a bridge on the Intracoastal Coastal Waterway in Nokomis, Pelican Alley Restaurant is rated the top restaurant in town. The building was constructed in 1945 and renovated several times. The current owners, Jeff and Renee, have been told over the years that a man haunts the place, which they found out right away. From the very beginning, things started happening.

The ghost is said to be the last owner and restaurateur, Robert Arbuckle Sr. He died the day before he was to sign the papers for Jeff and Renee to purchase the building and open their own restaurant. His wife signed the papers, but his spirit remains. To him, it's still the Admiral's Boardroom, his place.

Arbuckle is often seen in the kitchen door window, looking out into the dining area and making sure everyone is enjoying themselves. Objects are moved to different areas all the time, like someone is putting them in different places that he feels they should go and redoing the kitchen his way. He's seen

Pelican Alley. *Author's collection.*

sitting in the kitchen and prefers to make his appearances at night. He's a very playful character. People believe that he stops by to have drinks.

Doors open and close and footsteps are heard. Sometimes someone will get the feeling of being touched. Mediums come in to eat there and are always commenting on seeing a spirit sitting up by a ceiling ledge and being watched by this male spirit. Recently, the seawall started giving way, and they found huge cracks in kitchen area. This has now been fixed, and the site is back in business.

Update: Hurricane Irma did some damage to the restaurant. Our good thoughts and prayers are with them as they fix everything and get back up and running. Stop in and have great dinner and see if Mr. Arbuckle wants to have drink with you. And ask the staff for one of their stories. They all have one.

CONCLUSION

After the Depression and the ordeal of World War II, Bradenton and the surrounding areas flourished to become the thriving region it is today. Towns in Manatee County reflect a rich heritage of strong-willed people who have survived a challenging way of life.

While working on this book, we were supposed to take a direct hit from Hurricane Irma, just like years ago when we were supposed to take a direct hit from Hurricane Charlie. Both times the hurricanes turned below us. Most of us here believe that the legend of the Indians blessing this land to keep the storms away isn't a legend at all.

Many people have asked me how I became involved in the paranormal. Was it the death of my son? Well here's my Manatee County story. It starts when I was six years old and living in St. Paul, Minnesota. With the birth of my brother, we had outgrown our old house and needed to move into a new house. We had a nice yard, big trees and lots of kids to play with. My brother and I shared a room and slept in bunkbeds. I had the top, which my brother regretted the night I got sick.

My parents' room was across the hall, and my two older sisters shared a bedroom upstairs across from the huge attic. Now, the attic wasn't creepy, but I always had the feeling I was being watched. At night, I would hear footsteps that would come from the attic. Then the attic door would open, and the footsteps would start down the hallway to the stairs and continue down the stairs. From where I lay in my bed at night, I could see the door going to the upstairs open and close, and then the footsteps would continue

My childhood home. *Author's collection.*

to head into my room and stop right by the side of my bed. I could hear breathing but could not see anything. I'd pull the covers over my head and try to hide. Sometimes I had the feeling of someone holding the covers down and trying to suffocate me. I would panic and kick to get the covers off me. When I finally did get the covers off, I felt weak, like I had just fought for my life. This went on for a few years until my older sister moved out and I moved upstairs.

Right away, things started happening. I would hear the footsteps, the attic door would open and the footsteps would walk across the hall to our bedroom. Our door was always open, so the footsteps would come into room and I could feel something standing at the end of my bed staring at me. I knew then that I wasn't crazy and that I had the ability to feel and hear things others couldn't. I then noticed the spirit changing and sitting on my bed. I could see the imprint of someone sitting there but couldn't see anyone. Moving my leg to that spot felt like I was hitting someone sitting there.

One night, my sister and I had gotten into a loud argument, and our mom yelled up to us to stop it. We stepped out of the door, and I saw a man standing there. It was dark, and I thought it was my dad coming to quiet us down. I looked over the edge of stairs to see my dad standing next to my mom down at the bottom of the stairs. I looked back to where I saw the man, and he was gone.

Later, the attic was getting remodeled into a bedroom just for me. Before it was finished, I had started sleeping in there, and the male spirit would appear. I wasn't afraid anymore, so he didn't bother me. But after some communication between us, I found out that the spirit was the man who had built the house. His wife had died in the house, and he later took his own life.

Over the years, I have seen things that I've kept to myself and blocked as much as I could. However, occasionally, spirits would slip in, and I would notice them. In 1993, we moved to Bradenton, Florida. My husband's family had been living here since the 1920s, and we came down for a vacation and never wanted to leave. The beaches are beautiful, and it's sunny and a warm, friendly place to live. In 1997, I lost my eighteen-year-old son to cancer, and many feel that this must be why I got into paranormal investigation. In a way, it is, so I can prove to myself that there is really something out there after death—it would be a comfort to me to be with my son again. But in another way, it is to answer the questions of my experiences with the male spirit I shared a house with, the Confederate soldiers I've seen and the many more spirits I've encountered throughout my life.

Since my son died, we've had many other family members and loved ones pass away. One was my mother-in-law, Lorraine. She likes to let my daughter, Jamie, know that she's around and keeping an eye on her. Our dog, Theo, will start staring and barking at a corner in her room, and she'll say, "Grandma's here." I grab a K2 meter and go to her room and say, "Hi Lorraine," and nothing happens. My daughter will take meter and say, "Hi Grandma," and the K2 lights up to red, which is as high it can go. There has been contact with others in our house over the years, so I guess you could say that I live in a haunted house in Manatee County.

All of this has made me more aware of my abilities lately and has made me more aware of my son's presence. I may not be able to see him or talk to him, but I do feel every once in a while that he's giving me that special hug he'd give so I know he's there still.

I do often wonder about that male spirit in our original house. Two years ago, my daughter took me back to Minnesota. After forty years, I drove by that house, and there in the attic window was the male spirit standing looking out at me.

So there's my Manatee County story, which actually started in Minnesota when I was a child and continues on in Bradenton, Florida. I hope you enjoyed reading these stories as much as I enjoyed researching and listening to them being told to me. Whether you believe in spirits or not, legends and stories come from some type of truth.

Oh, and one last note. Most cemeteries have been shortened to make room for roads and sidewalks, so the pavement you are walking on could actually be someone's grave. Remember that when you are walking around. Please do check out some of these places or join us on one of our Bradenton Ghost Tours one night and talk to a few of these spirits. Please be respectful to the spirits, and they will respect you.

Resources

"Authentic Florida." Information available at the Eaton room, Manatee County Library.

Bradenton Herald.

Eaton Florida History Room, Manatee County Library. Interesting dates from Manatee County history.

Historical Venice Press. October 14, 2004.

"History of Manatee." Manatee County Library System, n.d.

Manatee County Carnegie Historical Library.

Manatee County Library.

Nash, Anna, curator. "Cortez Fisherman Women." *Bradenton Herald*, n.d. Written for the Maritime Museum.

Realize Bradenton. http://www.realizebradenton.com.

Interviews

Bassett, Kim, and Brandon Bassett. Interview by author, November 2017.

Mierkiewicz, Millie. Interview by author, December 20, 2016.

Wheeler, Jeff. Interview by author, October 2016.

ABOUT THE AUTHOR

L iz Reed was born and raised in St. Paul, Minnesota, for the first fifteen years of her life, and then moved to Texas. She currently lives in Bradenton, Florida, a west shore Florida "Friendly City." She is the founder of the Paranormal Society of Bradenton, Florida, and owner of the Downtown Bradenton & Bradenton Beach Ghost Tours. She had her first experience with spirits at the age of six. Since then, she has been drawn to find out more about what truly happens after death. She enjoys traveling with her daughter, Jamie, across the country, and they have many trips planned in the near future. Many include haunted locations. They just recently finished a trip to Savannah, Georgia, and are hoping for London next.